Smoking cessation training manual

A bio-behavioural approach to helping people to stop smoking

Emma Croghan

QUAY BOOKS

A division of MA Healthcare Ltd

Quay Books Division, MA Healthcare Ltd, St Jude's Church, Dulwich Road, London SE24 0PB

British Library Cataloguing-in-Publication Data
A catalogue record is available for this book

© MA Healthcare Limited 2007

ISBN-10: 1 85642 329 8
ISBN-13: 978 1 85642 329 8

Printed by Ashford Colour Press Ltd, Gosport, Cambridge

Note

Health care practice and knowledge are constantly changing and developing as new research and treatments, changes in procedures, drugs and equipment become available.

The author and publishers have, as far as is possible, taken care to confirm that the information complies with the latest standards of practice and legislation.

Contents

Contents

How to use this manual

This manual can be used either:

- In conjunction with a trainer in a formal classroom setting

or

- As a distance learning manual

Competence exercise

Before you read any further into the book, read each of the following statements and rate your current ability/competence to undertake the competency. Ratings are 1–5 (1 being novice and 5 being expert). These are adapted from the competencies developed by the UK Department of Health for facilitators of smoking cessation services.

Brief interventions

Competency	Rating
Ask about smoking in an appropriate way to elicit an accurate response	
Record status and action taken in an appropriate system	
Assess readiness to quit and willingness to use appropriate treatments	
Understanding and dissemination of the health risks of smoking and the benefits of quitting	
Understanding and describing the reasons why stopping smoking can be difficult	
Know what treatments are available to help with stopping smoking	
Know how to refer to local services	
Understanding of the wider context of smoking cessation	

Emma Croghan

One-to-one support and advice

Competence	Rating
Understand and describe national and local patterns of smoking behaviour as a function of age, gender, ethnic origin and social class	
Understand and describe behavioural and pharmacological determinants of smoking behaviour (including perceived benefits and disbenefits of smoking and quitting)	
Understand and demonstrate awareness of smoking cessation treatment methods, their effectiveness, appropriateness and evaluation	
Demonstrate the ability to assess a clients nicotine dependence, commitment to quit, past quit/smoking history, and the use of co monitors as a motivational, assessment and validatory tool	
Understand and be able to describe pharmacotherapy available to aid smoking cessation and demonstrate the ability to help clients choose the most appropriate supporting pharmacotherapy for each client	
Be able to offer appropriate, timely behavioural support	
Describe and plan appropriate treatment plans, aim, length, method and benefits	
Describe and plan monitoring and continuing education	

Group interventions

Competence	Rating
Describe potential difficulties in recruiting clients, and methods for dealing with these	
Demonstrate the ability to assess suitability for group treatment	
Demonstrate awareness of the logistics of running groups	
Plan and describe a treatment programme for groups	
Demonstrate awareness of short- and long-term results achieved in UK smoking cessation groups	
Demonstrate awareness of group processes and how they can help or hinder motivation to quit within the group	
Demonstrate awareness and strategies for dealing with 'problem' group members	
Plan and evaluate a method of keeping records of group attendance and outcome	
Show awareness of maintenance/relapse support systems	

Why does smoking matter?

Smoking matters because so many people do it. Although the prevalence of smoking has decreased steadily in the UK since the increasing publication of factual evidence about the health and other impacts of smoking, it has now stabilised. Around a quarter of all British adults currently smoke regularly (that is, every day). This figure increases with decreasing age, with around 30% of those aged under 65 smoking in the UK. Smoking rates are highest in those aged 20–24 (and in this age group young men are much more likely than young women to smoke – 36% and 29% respectively). Around a fifth of 15-year-olds smoke (more girls than boys at this age), but only 1% of 11-year-olds smoke. So most young people starting secondary school do not smoke, but by the age of 12 or 13 (1 to 2 years later) 40% have experimented, and by the age of 15, 60% have tried smoking. So smoking continues to be something which many people try (usually starting in adolescence) and continue to do into adulthood.

The number of people who do smoke would not be as relevant if it did not have wide-reaching social, physical and psychological impacts.

From a sociological perspective, smoking is more prevalent in areas and populations who are less affluent, with statistics showing increasing smoking levels with decreasing affluence. It has also been suggested that the health impact of smoking is more pronounced in those who are less affluent. Tobacco smoking is the main cause of the large inequality in health outcomes and life expectancy between the most and least affluent in society. There is now more public awareness and an increasing level of public health initiatives and legislation, such as smoke-free public places. Ireland became smoke-free in 2004 and Scotland in early 2006; England and Wales are due to enforce smoke-free public place policies in 2007. Smoke-free workplaces are another initiative which is being supported through policy, legislation and action. Because of these initiatives, smokers are increasingly feeling socially excluded, and this many be a factor in deciding to stop.

Physically, smoking is responsible for around 10% of all causes of mortality across the world. In the UK it is responsible for around 20% of all deaths – over 110,000 people every year, or over 300 per day. How many

Figure 1   Some risks associated with smoking.

seats were there on the last plane you travelled on? Or how many people work in your workplace? Less than or more than the number of people in the UK who die every day because of tobacco smoking?

In lifelong smokers, there is a 50% chance that eventual death will be smoking-related – and half of all these deaths will be premature, usually in middle age. By 2020, the World Health Organization (WHO) expects the worldwide death toll to reach 10 million, causing 17.7% of all deaths in developed countries – so it seems that smoking is not becoming less of an issue, but more of one. Tobacco smoking remains the single largest avoidable cause of premature death and disability in Britain.

Some of the increased physical risks associated with smoking are shown in Figure 1.

The psychology of smoking is fundamental to the issue. Social learning theory suggests that people learn to smoke from parents, peers and others, and we know that the risks of smoking are increased in those who have parents, siblings and friends who smoke. There is a very rapid brain response to each cigarette, which triggers a biological and chemical reward system so that people continue to smoke to achieve this positive sensation. Not only can it be viewed as a learned behaviour, but also as an associative behaviour, so that, much as Pavlov's dogs responded to a bell by salivating, people learn to associate smoking with pleasurable and relaxing activities and times, so the cigarettes become much more to them than dried leaves in a paper roll being burned and inhaled – they become iconic.

Smoking is a big issue around the world, again partly because so many people do it, but also because it is increasing in developing countries as tobacco companies move into previously unknown markets. Globally, more men than women smoke (47% and 12% respectively). In areas where very few women have smoked, significant increases in female smoking have recently been seen (in countries such as India, Cambodia and Malaysia).

The global impact of tobacco production is an often under-represented issue. Zimbabwe and Malawi both rely heavily on tobacco production (with over 50% of income from tobacco), although over 40 other developing countries also grow, cure and export the crop.

In most developing countries, the average price to a farmer per kilogram of tobacco ranges from 25–99p. A packet of cigarettes containing around 20 g of tobacco will make a clear profit of at least this much – giving tobacco companies huge profits.

The wider impact of smoking on the environment is seen in issues such as the number of trees felled to provide space for both growing and drying of tobacco (an area the size of the north of England each year), as well as

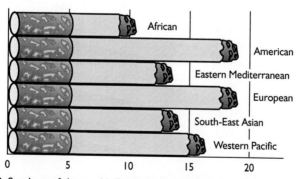

Figure 2 Smokers of the world. Figures represent number of cigarettes smoked per day, per daily smoker, by WHO region (Source: WHO, 1996).

the chemicals and fertilisers put onto tobacco crops to increase the yield per hectare.

Advertising

Tobacco is a heavily marketed product. Despite changes to the law in the UK from the late 1990s, restricting advertising of tobacco products at sporting events, on bill boards and in print, tobacco companies still spend large amounts on marketing their products. A survey a few years ago found that nearly 80% of American advertising executives from top agencies believed cigarette advertising *does* make smoking more appealing or socially acceptable to children (WHO, 2002). It is clear that tobacco advertising increases consumption in the following ways:

- By encouraging children and young people to experiment with tobacco and thereby slip into adult regular smoking
- By encouraging smokers to increase consumption
- By reducing smokers' motivation to quit
- By encouraging former smokers to resume the habit
- By discouraging full, open and honest discussion of the hazards of smoking
- 'By creating, through the ubiquity of advertising, sponsorship etc., an environment in which tobacco use is seen as familiar and acceptable and the warnings about its health are undermined' (United States Department of Health and Human Services, 1989).

The 56th World Health Assembly adopted the WHO Framework Convention on Tobacco Control unanimously on 21 May 2003 (http://www.who.int/tobacco/framework/en/). This framework requires four key areas of work for member states to achieve:

1. To take measures to protect all persons from exposure to tobacco smoke.
2. To take measures to prevent initiation of tobacco use, **to promote and support cessation** and to decrease the consumption of tobacco products in any form.
3. To take measures to promote the participation of indigenous individuals and communities in the development, implementation and evaluation of

tobacco control programmes which are socially and culturally appropriate to their needs and perspectives.
4. To take measures to address gender specific risks when delivering tobacco control initiatives.

To translate this into practice – as signatories to this policy, we need to:

1. Develop and implement wide smoke-free policies
2. Work with children and young people to prevent smiking uptake
3. Offer more stop smoking support
4. Involve our local populations in helping us to deliver the services that they want to use
5. Ensure that services are tailored to the needs of different gender smokers

National policy

Smoking Kills (Department of Health, 1998) is the UK government policy document, which sets clear health service targets for reducing levels of smoking in the population as a whole, and particularly amongst vulnerable groups: the young, pregnant women, and the disadvantaged. Smoking is known to be the principal avoidable cause of premature deaths in the UK. *Smoking Kills* was developed with the aim of reducing the mortality burden of smoking.

There is now a comprehensive NHS Stop Smoking Service, hosted or commissioned by primary care organisations offering support and help to smokers wanting to stop across the UK. Smoking cessation adjuncts nNicotine replacement therapy (NRT), bupropion (Zyban) and varenicline (Chantix) are available on NHS prescription to support this.

A network of local alliances for action on tobacco control has been established and there is a continuing programme of public advertising and awareness raising to persuade smokers to quit and non-smokers not to start.

The Quality and Outcomes Framework (QOF), part of the new general medical services (nGMS) contract for primary care services asks general practice services to collect information on how many people within certain disease areas smoke (CHD, stroke, hypertension, diabetes, COPD and asthma) and to undertake a brief intervention with these clients and record the outcome. It also requires smoking status to be recorded for a percentage of the practice population, and that brief interventions are offered to all identified smokers. Finally, it asks that smoking cessation be covered in any preconception care intervention. For these services a total of up to 68 QOF points are available.

'Prevalence of smoking' describes the number of people in the population at any one time who smoke. Three elements are required to reduce the prevalence of smoking:

1. Better prevention for children and young people to try to stop them becoming addicted to smoking tobacco.
2. An environment which supports not smoking as the social norm.

3. Better identification and treatment for people who want to stop smoking.

The four key target prevalence reduction areas stated in *Smoking Kills* are:

- To reduce smoking rates amongst all adults from 28% to 24% or less by 2010 (26% by 2005)
- To reduce smoking amongst manual groups from 32% to 26% or less by 2010 (29% by 2005)
- To reduce smoking amongst under 16s from 13% to 9% or less by 2010 (11%) by 2005
- To reduce smoking amongst pregnant women from 23% to 15% by 2010 (18% by 2005)

To achieve this, several action areas were identified for national government-led intervention:

- Smoking cessation services to be provided in each locality
- Tobacco advertising to end (magazine and billboard advertising banned April 2003)
- Media campaign to change attitudes to tobacco
- Campaign against tobacco smuggling
- Campaign for clean air in public places
- Codes of practice for workplace tobacco control
- Minimum international levels of tobacco taxation
- Protection of children and young people through restricting advertising in shops, under-age sales enforcement, and vending machine monitoring

However, as part of the Public Service Agreement (PSA) targets set as part of the H. M. Treasury spending review (2004), the following challenging target was set:

(PSA 3) Tackle the underlying determinants of ill health and health inequalities by:

Reducing adult smoking rates to 21% or less by 2010, with a reduction in prevalence among routine and manual groups to 26% or less.

The benefits of stopping smoking

Stopping smoking has both immediate and long-term health and social benefits. Within 20 minutes circulation improves, with blood pressure and pulse returning to normal levels. Within 8 hours, oxygen levels within the blood normalise, with the associated risk of a heart attack reduced. Within 24 hours, carbon monoxide (CO) is eliminated from the body.

With time, many of the long-term risks to health significantly reduce, in some cases returning to those of non smokers.

Stopping smoking has considerable financial benefits. With many people spending over £5 per packet of 20 cigarettes, the financial implications of this are clear. There are societal benefits too, as within 4–5 years following stopping smoking the use of NHS resources falls to at least those of a similar-aged non-smoker (Wagner *et al.*, 1995).

Sociologically and psychologically there are benefits, from no longer feeling that something has a hold and power over the client, to being able to socialise in non-smoking areas without the anxiety of needing to find somewhere to smoke.

Passive smoking

Around 15% of the smoke from cigarettes is consumed by the smokers themselves – the other 85% is released into the surrounding environment as 'side stream smoke'. Passive smoking (which may also be known as 'environmental tobacco smoke' (ETS) or 'second hand smoking') is a mixture of the smoke released from the burning of cigars, cigarettes or pipe tobacco and the smoke exhaled by the actual smoker.

There is no doubt that exposure to tobacco smoke is dangerous, whether the exposure is from being in a room or situation where tobacco smoke is entering the atmosphere, or from being a smoker. People who are regularly exposed to passive smoking have a 26% higher risk of heart disease and a 24% increased risk of lung cancer compared with people who are not regularly exposed to this type of smoke (ASH, 1999).

It is also important to note that passive smoking causes many health and social disadvantages for children who are exposed to this smoke in the home. They have higher risk of respiratory disease, and glue ear. They are also more likely to become smokers themselves.

Smoke-free policies and legislation relating to workplaces and 'public places' (restaurants, bars, public houses etc.) are developed precisely to reduce population exposure to this type of smoke.

Smoke free policies and services are important because:

- Passive smoking is hazardous to the health of non-smokers.
- Workers' rights, such as the inequality in terms of breaks and in terms of passive smoking. If you are a smoker, you will have on average an extra 50 minutes (usually paid) cigarette breaks each day compared with your non-smoking colleagues. This can cause disharmony at work and also promotes the idea that smoking is beneficial, as we are rewarding people who smoke with extra paid breaks whilst simultaneously penalising those who do not smoke.
- Non-smokers' rights – relating to exposure to environmental tobacco smoke. It is everyone's right to have a choice about whether they smoke or not, but when smokers are in enclosed areas and non-smokers are around, the choice of the non-smoker is compromised.

- The focus with any smoke-free policy should be on *where* and *when*, rather than *whether*, people smoke.

'Smoke-free' is not about a nanny state and social control, but about equality and offering everyone choices and opportunities for health and social well-being. Stop smoking support is not about *making* people stop smoking, but is about offering informed and rational choices to people.

Socialisation to smoking

Socialisation is the process by which individuals learn to partake of the attitudes, values and behaviours of a society or community. Primary socialisation, which occurs in early childhood, is usually based on family and societal norms within the familial or cultural environment. Secondary socialisation is the process of learning appropriate behaviour for a smaller (often peer- and friendship-led) group of a wider societal group – this is usually noticed in adolescence and is often part of individualisation. Finally, of note here is the process of anticipatory socialisation, which refers to the processes of socialisation in which a person 'rehearses' for future positions, occupations and social relationships.

Primary socialisation theories led us to suggestions that changing behaviours in childhood can lead to healthy behaviours through life. These periods of socialisation are important to explain lifestyle choices, in both early and later childhood, and partially explain why it is important to intervene early to imbue children with the knowledge, attitudes and behaviours of a healthy lifestyle at an early age, as well as reinforcing them through environmental norms as part of primary socialisation.

This reduces the impact of the power of other authorities to make the lifestyle choices for a young child as, when they are able, the primary and secondary socialisation which has occurred through reinforcement of the healthy lifestyle choice through the environment will lead to them being increasingly likely to take the healthy choice.

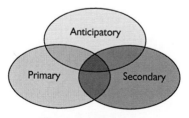

Figure 3 Socialisation.

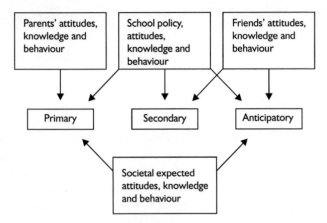

Figure 4 Social marketing affecting attitudes, knowledge and behaviour.

Fitness, looking good and smoking cessation

Cigarette smoking affects the appearance in a negative way, causing smokers to look older than non-smokers of the same age. Skin is more likely to wrinkle, as elastin is damaged and because of the long-term facial expressions which go alongside smoking (squinting, lip pursing). Staining of hands and teeth from continued exposure to tar, and dry and dull skin, are all side-effects of smoking which may impact upon self-esteem.

Male smokers are more likely to suffer from impotence, and in women the menopause is likely to be experienced around two years earlier than for non-smokers.

There is some evidence to suggest that exercise can be beneficial as a supportive adjunct to stopping smoking. It seems that it may help in maintaining a quit attempt in a number of ways. In one study, participating in exercise-based activity for the 12 weeks immediately following a quit attempt led to double the chances of stopping smoking and staying stopped, with a much reduced weight gain (Marcus *et al.*, 2005).

The most recent evidence suggests that even if exercise advice and support does not aid smoking cessation, it does aid the psychological problems associated with withdrawal from nicotine addiction (Usher *et al.*, 2003).

Weight gain and smoking

Many people are concerned about gaining weight on stopping smoking. Up to 80% of quitters put on some weight when quitting. This weight gain usually ranges from 4.5 to 7 lb, but in 13% of women and 10% of men, weight gains in excess of 28 lb have been seen. The consequence of this is that weight gain is an important barrier to smoking cessation, particularly in women. A recent survey of new clients presenting to a local stop smoking service asked if they were worried about putting on weight. Sixty per cent of men and 80% of women said this was an important factor and that they were concerned about it. This concern is further supported by the fact that around 80% of stop smoking service clients relapse within twelve months of trying to stop smoking, often citing the weight gain as the main reason for the relapse.

Take the example of Joanne – a practice facilitator who smoked and had Type 2 diabetes. She tried and successfully stopped smoking for a period of three months (12 weeks), by which point she had gained *2 stones* in weight, and her HbA1C (marker of diabetes) was rising at an alarming rate. She felt unwell and was unhappy with her appearance and the fact that she had had to purchase a whole new set of clothes. She described her experience:

> I was very unhappy with how much weight I was putting on – I kept seeing my doctor about how unwell I felt; much of it seemed to be related to my worsening diabetes. I know how it feels to have diabetes and feel unwell, but I don't know how it feels to have lung cancer, or something like that... so I thought about it, weighed it up, and decided to start smoking again... and now my HbA1C is OK and I lost the weight.

Post-smoking cessation weight gain has been associated with a reduction in energy expenditure of up to 100 kcal/day, accounting for approximately one-third of the weight gain after smoking cessation. Two thirds of the weight gain relates to increased intake of food. The increased intake of food, in turn, relates to not feeling full so quickly. When eating, the stomach stretches, and at the point of 'full' stretch a hormone called leptin is secreted in the brain. Leptin is an appetite inhibitor, which signifies satiety (fullness), and so the person stops eating. When people stop smoking, the brain becomes less sensitive to leptin, so they eat more because they do not feel full.

It is possible for people to stop smoking without experiencing significant (or indeed, any) weight gain. This is usually supported through the use of some of a number of activities such as:

- Making sure healthy snacks are available (fruit and vegetables)
- Drinking more water during the quit attempt
- Being more active (if you are already active, you can choose to increase the duration, the frequency or the intensity of your current activity)
- If craving sweet foods, try fruit, such as bananas, or sugar-free chewing gum

Managing weight gain, through offering access to activity or exercise, through awareness and through other supportive mechanisms can help and is an important way of showing a client-sensitive service – if a client is worried about weight gain, the service offered would not be holistic if it did not offer mechanisms to reduce this concern.

Pharmacies and smoking cessation

The involvement of pharmacies in public health, and in supporting the achievement of key public health targets aimed at improving population health and increasing choice to consumers has been debated over the past few years (Asghar *et al.*, 2002; Anderson *et al.*, 2003; Department of Health, 2003).

This has recently been formalised with the introduction of a contractual framework for community pharmacies with clear and specific guidance for PCTs to engage with them to achieve public health targets and outcomes (Department of Health, 2005). Stop smoking services can be commissioned by PCTs or by other commissioners as part of a Local Enhanced Service (LES) provided by volunteering community pharmacies. Given the number, location and opening times of community pharmacies across a given area, this represents a large increase in the potential capacity of the public health workforce.

The use of patient group directives (PGDs) can ensure that local organisations work together to offer choices of service providers to clients, so that they can receive some pharmacological adjuncts as well as behavioural support within the services delivered by pharmacies.

Nicotine and stress

Many smokers describe smoking as stress-relieving, but often stopping smoking can be much more stress-relieving, as many of the anxieties experienced by smokers about money, health and other factors, such as social stigmatisation, are reduced.

Nicotine stimulates the brain to release dopamine, which is associated with pleasurable feelings, and smokers quickly develop regular smoking patterns. Eventually, smokers need increasing levels of nicotine to feel 'normal'. As the nicotine content in their blood drops below a certain level, they begin to crave for a cigarette. This craving makes the smoker feel 'stressed'. If we add on the breaks/time out/deep breathing, then of course smokers talk abut a stress reduction following a cigarette.

Consider Louise, a young office worker in a small company. Louise perceives her job to be stressful, and manages this partly by smoking. Smoking allows her to go outside for a period of around ten minutes, several times a day (she averages 4–6 breaks per day, depending on how 'stressful' a day it is). So on an average day, Louise has 50 minutes' extra paid breaks than she would normally have. If she stopped smoking these breaks would not happen. When she goes outside for a break, she takes several deep breaths to inhale deeply of her cigarette, dropping her shoulders as she exhales. She talks with her friends who also smoke and sees it as a pleasant interlude in her working day.

Practical example

Put your hand on the top of your stomach. Does it move in and out with your breathing? Now take a big deep breath in – try to fill your lungs to their capacity. Now does your stomach move? This deep breathing is very relaxing (it is known as diaphramagtic breathing and is often used in yoga and Pilates as a relaxing mechanism). When people smoke they do this 10–15 times per cigarette!

Exercise 1: Reflection

Does your employer condone smoking by allowing smoking breaks but not allowing the same amount of breaks for non-smokers? Is there anything which the company or organisation can do to reduce this inequality, which may inherently reward smoking and punish not smoking?

Cigarette smoking and health

Mental health

Cigarette smoking is linked with a wide range of psychiatric diagnoses, including:

- Anxiety
- Agoraphobia
- Panic disorder
- Depression and bipolar disorder
- Schizophrenia

It has been shown that clients who experience depressive episodes, phobias or obsessive compulsive disorders are at least twice as likely as those with none of these disorders to smoke (Coultard *et al.*, 2000). Having more than one disorder significantly increases the likelihood of smoking.

Depression has been shown to be both affective to and affected by smoking. Some research (Breslau *et al.*, 1998) indicates that clients with depression are more likely to smoke than those without, whilst other research has demonstrated an increased risk of depressive symptoms and increased risk of severe depression in daily smokers. It seems that nicotine may act as an anti-depressant in some smokers and could therefore be viewed as a form of self-medication.

This is because every cigarette provides an acute release of serotonin but at the same time long term cigarette smoking leads to chronic decrease in brain serotonin levels. This leads to increased need for cigarettes to stabilise mood. A history of depression may result in increased depressive symptoms and, serious major depression may ensue in quitters.

Some people believe that smoking itself could act as a trigger for mental illness. Alternatively, as we have seen, people diagnosed with a mental illness are at much higher risk of smoking than others.

Nicotine dependence itself is classified as a mental disorder from which most smokers suffer. This dependence is strongly associated with a variety of other mental health disorders.

Mental health service users are more likely to smoke and are less likely to stop smoking, for a number of reasons. They are less likely to be offered support to stop smoking, and also often find it harder to stop smoking.

Other key issues relating to smoking and mental health are:

- Smoking cigarettes interacts with neuroleptic treatment (drug treatment for schizophrenics), reducing neuroleptic plasma levels and possibly causing higher doses of neuroleptics to be prescribed.
- Nearly all mental health drug therapy reduces the biological urge to smoke, but when on the neuroleptic haloperidol people smoke more.
- Research suggests smoking may accelerate cognitive decline in non-demented elderly.

Mortality

Patients with severe mental health problems have a higher risk of premature death than the general population. Having a mental disorder predicts an elevated risk of death from cardiovascular disease, coronary heart disease, respiratory disease and suicide.

Smoking causes elevated risks from both cardiovascular and respiratory diseases. It seems that the combination of some drug therapies used in mental health, and lifestyle issues such as smoking, are likely to be the causal factors in this.

Finance

People can spend a large proportion of their income on smoking.

Many people with mental health problems often live on a very low income, and the money spent on cigarettes is then not available to spend on clothing, leisure pursuits and personal possessions that could help to improve their quality of life.

Physical health

Physical health is often under supported in mental health service users through general practice and non-mental health services.

Despite a reasonably high GP consultation rate, people with severe mental illness are much less likely than the general population to be offered health promotion interventions such as smoking cessation.

Drug therapy

Patients who are stable on any drug metabolised by CYP1A2, and who smoke but then stop, can have toxic levels appear in their blood over a matter of days as less of the drug is metabolised.

Exacerbation of mental health symptoms has not been detected on attempting abstinence. A recent review of smoking bans in mental health and addiction settings (Lawn and Pols, 2005) indicates that total or partial smoking bans resulted in 'no major long-standing untoward effects in terms of behavioural indicators of unrest of compliance'. A second study showed the apprehensions of staff and patients dissipated with time after the smoking ban was implemented.

Table 1 shows a list of drugs that may need dose adjustments when a patient stops smoking.

Table I

BNF category Drug name/class	Nature of interaction	Dose in smokers	Management when stopping smoking
2.3 Flecainide	Serum levels may be lower in smokers.	Smokers may need larger doses.	The dose of flecainide is adjusted according to response. If a patient taking flecainide stops smoking, the minimum effective dose might be reduced.
2.4 Beta-blockers	Smoking can reduce the effect of beta-blockers on blood pressure and heart rate. Smokers may have reduced serum levels of propranolol.	Smokers may need larger doses, depending upon response.	The dose of a beta-blocker is adjusted according to response. If a patient taking beta-blockers stops smoking, the dose may need to be reduced. Monitor blood pressure.
2.8 Warfarin	Smoking may slightly increase warfarin metabolism.	Dose requirements may be slightly increased.	The dose of warfarin is adjusted according to each patient's International Normalised Ratio (INR). If a patient taking warfarin stops smoking, the INR may increase. Advise patients to tell the physician managing their anticoagulant control that they are stopping smoking.
3.1 Theophylline	In smokers the half-life of theophylline is reduced and elimination is considerably more rapid, due to induction of enzyme CYP1A2.	Smokers need higher doses. For heavy smokers the dose may need to be doubled.	The dose of theophylline will need to be reduced if a patient stops smoking or is admitted to hospital and unable to smoke. Prodigy guidance on smoking cessation advises that plasma theophylline concentrations should be monitored and the dose of theophylline adjusted accordingly (usually about a week after withdrawal). The dose of theophylline will typically need to be reduced by about a third. Advise the patient to seek help if they develop signs of theophylline toxicity such as palpitations or nausea.

Table 1 (continued)

BNF category Drug name/class	Nature of interaction	Dose in smokers	Management when stopping smoking
4.1 Benzodiazepines and zolpidem	These medicines possibly have less hypnotic effect in smokers due to central nervous system (CNS) stimulation from smoking.	The clinical significance of this interaction is not clear.	Patients taking benzodiazepines or zolpidem may experience increased sedation after giving up smoking. If so, the dose should be reduced.
4.2 Chlorpromazine and fluphenazine	Serum levels may be lower in smokers.	Smokers may need larger doses.	Patients taking chlorpromazine or fluphenazine may require smaller doses after stopping smoking. Consider dose reduction if a patient suffers adverse effects such as drowsiness or extra-pyramidal side effects.
4.2 Clozapine	Serum levels may be lower in smokers.	Smokers may need larger doses.	If a patient taking clozapine stops smoking, the dose may need to be reduced. Advise the patient to inform their psychiatrist that they are stopping smoking.
4.2 Haloperidol and olanzapine	Serum levels may be lower in smokers.	Smokers may need larger doses.	Patients taking haloperidol or olanzapine may require smaller doses after stopping smoking. Consider dose reduction if a patient suffers adverse effects such as drowsiness or extra-pyramidal side effects.
4.9 Ropinirole	Ropinirole is metabolised via CYP1A2 so elimination may be more rapid in smokers.	Smokers may need larger doses.	Theoretically, if a patient taking ropinirole stops smoking, the dose may need to be reduced.

Table 1 (continued)

BNF category Drug name/class	Nature of interaction	Dose in smokers	Management when stopping smoking
6.1 Insulin	Smokers who have insulin-dependent diabetes may need more insulin than non-smokers.	Dose is adjusted according to individual need.	If a patient with insulin-dependent diabetes stops smoking, their dose of insulin may need to be reduced. Advise the patient to be alert for signs of hypoglycaemia and to test their blood glucose more frequently.
9.5 Cinacalcet	Serum levels are lower in smokers.	Smokers may need larger doses.	If a patient taking cinacalcet stops smoking, the dose may need to be reduced. Advise the patient to inform their nephrologist when they stop smoking. Monitor parathyroid hormone levels and adjust the dose accordingly.

From: UKMi Q&A 136.1 Which medicines need dose adjustment when a patient stops smoking? Expiry: 31st March. 2008druginfo@liv.ac.uk

Cigarette smoking and pregnancy

Around 17% of pregnant women in the UK currently smoke regularly.

Most women make an attempt to change their smoking behaviour during pregnancy, by either cutting down or stopping smoking. Around 14% quit prior to pregnancy, whilst 64% quit/reduce during pregnancy (70% of these in the first 10 weeks). Around one in ten will start smoking, or will return to their previous levels of smoking, before the birth. Over half (52%) of partners of a pregnant woman change their behaviour, reducing or stopping smoking during the pregnancy. Forty per cent of women who smoke report that their partner has asked them to change their smoking habit, although there is no evidence that the women themselves find this supportive or helpful to changing their behaviour (HDA, 2003). Smoking in pregnancy is most common in women who are younger at conception, single, of lower educational achievement or in unskilled occupations.

Smoking in pregnancy is dangerous to the baby, the pregnancy and the mother. Some key facts:

- Babies born to mothers who smoke are lighter by 200 g (average). Paternal smoking also results in lighter babies.
- There is a 25% increase in miscarriage amongst pregnant smokers.
- Babies are shorter and have smaller head circumference.
- There is a 33% increase in perinatal mortality.
- Smoking in pregnancy results in long-term reduction in growth and educational achievement of the child.
- There is some evidence that suggest that children born to mothers who smoke are at statistically higher risk of obesity at school age.

Targets relating to smoking in pregnancy are inherent in current policy and strategy. Smoking cessation has been identified as a key target area within Sure Start: for example, an initial target for Sure Start was, for fully operational programmes, by March 2006 – 'a 6 percentage point reduction in the proportion of mothers who continue to smoke during pregnancy'. Within the English Department of Health targets is the aspiration:

'To reduce smoking amongst pregnant women from 23% to 15% by 2010 (18% by 2005)'.

All pregnant women and their partners should be asked about smoking, *but* it should be in a non-judgemental, non-threatening manner, which is perceived as being supportive by the woman and/or her partner, for example: 'Have you ever tried to stop smoking?' or 'What do you think about smoke-free?'.

Cigarette smoking and adolescence

Adolescence is a transitional time, spanning the period from around 10 years old until 18 or 19, in which major physiological, social, psychological and cognitive changes take place. It signals the change from child to adult, and is often a time of stress, mental and physical turbulence and confusion, and a time when the young person may challenge the rules and norms around them in a bid to define themselves as individuals. This period of life is such a dramatic one that it is difficult to class all adolescents as the same, as a young person of 10 is developmentally different from an 18-year-old. It is therefore useful to theoretically split adolescence into three phases: early (aged 10 to 13), middle (13 to 15) and late adolescence (15 to 19). Throughout their adolescence, young people are striving to enhance their sense of self. They do this by asking themselves four main questions (Perkins, 2001):

1. 'Who am I?'. This is often to do with defining the sexual and social being – do I need to smoke to fulfil this?
2. 'Am I normal?'. Do I fit in with those who I like and admire? Do they smoke, and therefore should I?
3. 'Am I competent and useful?'. Am I good at something which others value? Am I able to smoke competently and confidently?
4. 'Am I lovable/loving?'. Can someone other than my family love me and can smoking help with this?

When health professionals work with adolescents, they need to have an understanding of this wider context which is of fundamental importance to the young person and which may prompt them to undertake activities and roles which may be damaging to health in the long or short term.

Risk taking is the willingness to make mistakes, to advocate unconventional or unpopular positions, or to tackle extremely challenging problems without obvious solutions, such that one's personal growth, integrity or accomplishments are enhanced. The very nature of learning requires risk taking. A child would never learn to walk, talk or socially interact without taking risks, experiencing successes and failures, and then monitoring and adjusting behaviours accordingly.

Risk taking can be understood as 'going against the social or cultural norm' as much as a reference to problematic or health-decreasing risk. In fact, when talking about 'risk taking' in relation to young people, we are often talking about health-detracting behaviours such as truancy, smoking or participating in extreme sports. The usual definition of risk taking, when applied to children and young people, tends to trigger an impression of taking a chance that something bad will happen as a result of the decision that is made to take the risk.

Amongst young people, tobacco smoking is defined as at least one cigarette per week (Boreham *et al.*, 2003). National rates of regular smoking vary by age and over time, peaking in 1996 with an overall average of 13% and falling thereafter to an overall average of 9% in 1999. This rises to 10% in 2000 and remains at 10% in 2001 (Boreham *et al.*, 2003; Department of Health, 2004) and drops to 9% in 2003 (Boreham *et al.*, 2003; Department of Health, 2004, 2005). Girls are more likely to be regular smokers than boys (11% compared with 9%) and regular smoking increases sharply with age. One per cent of all 11-year-olds were regular smokers in 2002 compared with 22% of 15-year-olds. The proportion of young people who have ever smoked reached a peak in 1984 at 55% and has followed a downward trend since, with 44% of girls and 39% of boys in 2002 described this way (Boreham *et al.*, 2002). Most adult smokers in the UK commenced their smoking habit before the age of 16 (82%) and nearly two thirds (63%) of 16-year-olds have tried smoking or still are smokers (Jarvis, 1997).

Adolescent smoking poses a concern because of the numbers and proportions of young people who begin smoking in adolescence and then go on to become long-term adult smokers (around 50%), thus affecting their life chances. There are correlations between smoking prevalence and community deprivation indices for adult smokers, but there is no social class difference amongst adolescents who experiment with smoking (Croghan *et al.*, 2003). There is, however, a large social class differentiation between those who go on to become adult smokers. Those in lower socio-economic groups have an increased risk of becoming long-term smokers (HDA, 2003). This group is also more likely to go on to suffer increased rates of morbidity and lower mortality rates from their smoking than do their counterparts in other socio-economic groups. It can be argued that this increases inequalities, not just around health but also around wealth, with smokers in the lowest socio-economic groups spending a higher proportion of their household income on cigarettes than other groups.

Among young people, the short-term health effects of smoking include damage to the respiratory system, addiction to nicotine and, arguably, the associated risk of other drug use. The potential long-term health consequences of youth smoking are reinforced by the fact that around half of young people who smoke regularly continue to smoke throughout adulthood.

Carbon monoxide and smoking

Carbon monoxide (CO) is a gas which is delivered to smokers through smoking cigarettes. It is a highly toxic, colourless and odourless gas which binds effectively with haemoglobin, reducing oxygen capacity. This is most damaging to health when lung function or oxygen capacity is already impaired or at times of extra burden and physical/chemical stress to the body (e.g. during pregnancy).

The physical effects of high CO levels over a prolonged period of time, such as the chronic high levels found in long-term smokers, include chest pain, abdominal pain and genito-urinary disturbance, nausea and vomiting, dizziness, visual disturbance, lethargy and headaches.

Carbon monoxide levels are measured as 'parts per million (ppm)' and levels of more than 50 ppm are considered hazardous to health – sufficiently so that this level could close a building under health and safety legislation. Levels in tobacco smoke range from 1–50,000 ppm.

CO readings can be a useful motivational tool to support a stop smoking attempt, as clients can see for themselves the effects of stopping smoking. Levels of CO from one cigarette are elevated and can be seen using a CO monitor for up to 24 hours after cigarette consumption. Within 24 hours of stopping smoking, levels should be that of a non-smoker.

Although there are several manufacturers of CO monitors, most have similar instructions and interpretations. Care should be taken, when using these machines, that you are following the correct interpretation levels. The table below shows a rough guide.

CO level (ppm)	Interpretation
0–5	Non-smoker
6–10	Usually a non-smoker in an area with high environmental CO levels – although in adolescence, this may indicate cigarette smoking
11–low 70s	Smoker
Mid 70s+	Toxic levels

To use a CO machine, a single-use tube should be attached to the monitor. The client should be instructed to take a deep breath in and hold for 10–15 seconds (varies with machines) whilst the machine counts down the seconds. Breath is held to allow for equilibrium with alveolar air to be achieved. On 3 seconds, the client should seal their lips around the tube and at 0 seconds should blow out one long, exhalation into the tube. The machine will then display the results in ppm of carbon monoxide.

Service provision

The types of services available to clients are based on evidence and best practice guidance developed and published from the late 1990s (Raw *et al.*, 1998; West *et al.*, 2000; NICE, 2006). Clinical guidelines for smoking cessation published in the journal *Thorax* in December 1998 and updated in December 2000 reviewed the evidence base and set out recommended treatments. The guidelines were based on the evidence provided by authoritative reviews. The guidelines show that brief advice, backed up by a prescription for NRT or bupropion, and referral to specialist support where needed, greatly increases the smoker's ability to stop smoking. The guidance suggests that smoking cessation support can be offered at the following levels, and by the following types of service providers:

- Brief opportunistic advice to stop smoking – this should be offered by all health care professionals in line with *Thorax* and National Institute for Health and Clinical Excellence (NICE) guidance (NICE, 2006)
- One-to-one behavioural support to aid quit attempts (general practice facilitator, occupational health advisors, health visitors, pharmacists or community facilitators, school facilitators etc., with or without pharmacological support)
- Specialist services to aid quit attempts (support groups or one-to-one counselling, with or without pharmacological support)

There are an estimated 2.5–5% of smokers who do succeed in stopping on their own. Health care professionals play a crucial role by initiating and motivating quit attempts. More intensive specialist support is particularly important for highly dependent smokers, disproportionately found in the lowest income groups, who are not able to stop with brief interventions. Intensive specialist support offered along the lines of the evidence base, together with NRT or bupropion, offers the highest cessation rates. The efficacy of the interventions varies.

Brief advice from a health professional routinely given to all patients who smoke leads to about 40% attempting to stop and about 5% stopping for at least six months (a strong predictor of permanent success). Face-to-face behavioural support from a cessation specialist enables about

10% to succeed in the long term, double the effect of a brief intervention. For pregnant smokers, this type of support has a similar level of success, about 10% long term. However, the most effective support relates to intensive behavioural support, either one-to-one or group, plus pharmacological support, enabling about 20% to stop long term at up to 12 months. Broadly, the more support offered and taken, the better the outcome for the smoker.

Brief interventions

A brief intervention will take around 5–10 minutes, and smoking may be a side issue which comes up in conversation, rather than the focus of the whole visit or intervention. The following areas need to be covered in the intervention so that accurate data can be collected. This is mainly so that:

1. The smoking status of all patients/clients can be established in an appropriate way to elicit an accurate response.
2. All smokers can be assessed to identify appropriate smokers who might be receptive to messages pertaining to wanting to quit, ensuring that information is provided which talks about the major health risks of smoking and the benefits to health of quitting, and acknowledging that quitting can be difficult.
3. All smokers can be assessed to identify their receptivity to the practicalities of quitting depending upon the cues the client provides in response to 'soft' enquiries (i.e. the client provides a positive or interested response, suggesting a 'go on?' response).
4. If the client provides a response which demonstrates interest in more information, assist the smoker to consider quitting: this is best achieved through providing a 'menu' which aims to describe treatments available to help with stopping smoking in the locality. The overarching aim of this is to support informed choice.
5. If informed choice suggests that the client would like more information and would like a referral to further services, arrange referral to local services or follow-up. Where possible, ask the client to facilitate the next appointment (thereby putting the onus on them to demonstrate an interest in quitting).

A key outcome of a brief intervention is the provision of supportive (and self help) literature for the client (NICE, 2006; West *et al.*, 2000).

Example protocol for brief intervention

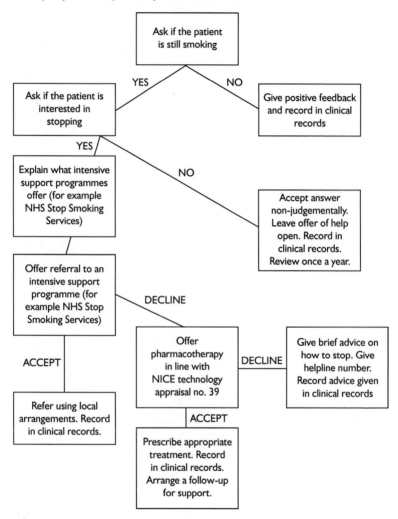

Figure 5 NICE (2006) guidance for diagrammatic representation of brief intervention and outcomes.

One-to-one support

This service is provided for smokers who have come forward and requested help with quitting, but are unable to or unwilling to access or utilise specialist services. It is for service users who have experienced a brief intervention and decided that they do want to make a stop smoking attempt, or for those who are both interested in and motivated to try to stop smoking. Clients can access this service in a number of ways, depending on the locality – they may self refer or be referred through another worker (such as a health care professional who has delivered a brief intervention).

The minimum standards expected for this level of service are:

- Smokers should be seen at multiple contacts over a period of weeks, usually ranging from 8 to 12.
- An assessment of:
  - What is the client's commitment to the present quit attempt?
  - What is the client's past smoking and quitting history?
  - What are the perceived benefits of smoking to the client?
  - What are the perceived disbenefits of smoking to the client?
  - What withdrawal symptoms can the client expect, and what can you do about them?
  - What is the right pharmacological support for this client?
  - What side effects can they expect?
- Monitoring of the client's quit attempt

This level of service is offered by nurses, pharmacists and other stop smoking advisors who have all been trained to deliver both the biological and behavioural support required by a client. The following have also been suggested as the basis of a high-quality smoking cessation service provision (Department of Health, 2004b; West *et al.*, 2003):

- An initial consultation lasting twenty to thirty minutes involving assessment of motivation and readiness to stop, setting a quit date, and advice on and provision of NRT or bupropion if appropriate.
- Follow-up at twelve months from the quit date to assess if the patient is still not smoking; this can be done by telephone (with abstinent patients subsequently coming in for measurement of expired air CO for validation).

Example one-to-one protocol

This protocol is just one example of the services provided in a one-to-one service, but should only be used as a framework and should not be seen in isolation of client need – it can therefore be used as a basic level of service provision. Second appointment refers to post brief intervention.

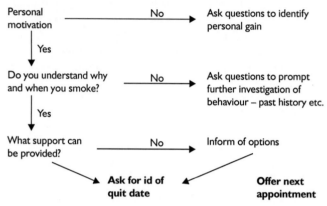

Figure 6 Second appointment (20–30 minutes). What did you find out about yourself – triggers, feelings etc?

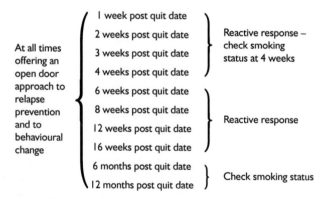

Figure 7 Quit date reached. Contact 1–3 days later – check OK?

Group support

This type of service is usually offered by organisations (workplaces, primary care organisations, voluntary organisations, schools etc.) and provides behavioural support in groups for smokers who have identified a wish to quit. Groups offer intensive support over a number of weeks. They are usually free if run through the local Stop Smoking Service or NHS. Over a number of weeks, the group facilitator leads the participants through the self-assessment and understanding, planning, implementation and evaluation of the quit attempt.

When considering facilitating a group, it is important to consider the following factors:

1. How could you assess and recruit clients to your service? Do you have posters or adverts, or are you using word of mouth? What is your referral pathway?
2. What will you do at each session? How fluid will it be?
3. Some members, usually those who are less motivated to quit themselves, or those who feel pressured to quit (they may feel they have been 'sent'), can be 'difficult' to manage and can be disruptive both to the group members and to the group dynamic.
4. How can you ensure that clients are monitored when the group is no longer meeting?

Principles of delivering groups

The group should be run as an informal group with between 10 and 16 members, although there are no hard and fast rules. The venue should be one which is acceptable to the participants, which is perceived as friendly and which they are comfortable visiting. The facilitator for the group should be friendly, enthusiastic and welcoming and should feel able to support all members of the group, even if they do not stop smoking.

The facilitator should arrive at least 10 minutes prior to the group starting, in time to organise chairs and drinks. Wherever possible, light refreshments should be provided.

Everything discussed in the group is considered to be confidential to and within the group. All group members should be offered respect and should not be made fun of or teased.

It is important to consider the level of group dynamics. Consider how much time the facilitator spends talking – the aim should be to keep facilitator-led talking to around 30–40%, with 60–70% of discussions being provided by participants.

Other health behaviours and behaviour change

Often clients present to smoking cessation services with other health behaviours that they would like to address. These may be related to:

- Soft drug use (particularly inhaled drugs such as cannabis)
- Obesity or overeating
- Exercise
- Other behaviours which clients may consider they wish to change

The principles of behaviour change described throughout this book are transferable to other behaviours.

However, changing behaviour such as smoking may be stressful and difficult for clients. They (and you!) may find it easier to concentrate on one 'problem' issue at a time. For example, if a client is concerned about their weight and their smoking, but is ready to change their smoking behaviour, it may be most appropriate to deal with the smoking first, followed by the weight issue. This is not always the case – some people make multiple changes more successfully than single issues – but service providers should be flexible enough to respond to a number of issues at once, whilst acknowledging that this is not appropriate for some people.

Social marketing, young people and socialisation

Social marketing has been referred to as 'the application of marketing to the solution of health and social problems' (MacFadyen *et al.*, 1999). The most commonly held definition of social marketing is 'the design, implementation and control of programs [*sic*] calculated to influence the acceptability of social ideas and involving considerations of product planning, pricing, communication, distributions and market research' (Kotler and Zaltman, 1971).

Social marketing can therefore be used as the framework for understanding and influencing human behaviour and decision-making processes. The white paper *Choosing Health, Making Healthier Choices Easier* (Department of Health, 2004c) suggests that there is a significant role for health services to play in marketing the idea of positive health choices to clients. A specialist unit has been set up within the Department of Health (the Social Marketing Development Unit) to integrate a social marketing approach within key work streams, specifically including healthy schools and the public health of children and young people, as well as wider public health issues such as alcohol, tobacco and other drug use and misuse, nutrition, physical activity and health inequalities.

This is an important role for health professionals, working to affect socialisation so that people subconsciously choose to make healthy choices wherever possible. It must not be forgotten that health services work with a group of people who are a very important target market to anti-health forces – and these forces are very keen on affecting brand identity in children and young people to claim them as customers for life.

Young people and smoking

Marketing to young people is an essential element of influencing socialisation, brand and lifestyle choices. The biggest toy manufacturer and distributor in the UK (indeed, in the world) is McDonald's (Pauli, 2006). The tobacco companies have identified 13–18-year-olds as *replacement smokers* – to replace the chronic smokers who die, on average 10 years prematurely (and so become a lost market, and loss of ten years' profits) (ASH, 2006).

There are several stages to an approach (from the Department of Health's Social Marketing Unit) which socially markets not smoking and a stop smoking service:

1. Establishing behavioural goals which are measurable and specific – i.e. not smoking.
2. Consumer research and pre-testing – knowledge of the needs and identities of the client group. What motivates them to smoke? What might motivate them to stop? What service configuration is most appropriate – groups, one-to-one or something else, such as email or test-based support?
3. Segmentation and targeting – offering different options and services to different groups within the client sector, such as one-to-one, groups, home-based services and virtual options.
4. Marketing mix – using different methods and mechanisms to establish the service: location, cost implications, advertising etc.
5. The exchange approach – supporting clients through knowledge (usually gained in Stage 1) of what motivates them and the potential costs and benefits to the clients from their perspective. In other words, selling not smoking based on what clients want to gain from not smoking.
6. Dealing with competition – what other competing external or internal market forces exist (mainly the pull back to smoking, including marketing of tobacco).

All clients are individuals and will have a different trigger for change to increase receptivity.

Exercise 2

What might you need to think about, in terms of social marketing for the following groups in your area of work:

1. Men
2. Women
3. Adolescents
4. Workers
5. Black and ethnic minorities
6. Mental health
7. Geographical areas of deprivation?

How will you recruit your target groups to your service?

How to talk to people about stopping smoking

Sometimes it is very difficult to talk to clients about smoking. Smoking is a *bio-behavioural* issue, and the rituals and comforts that clients derive from smoking are hard to understand, appreciate and change. The right approach can facilitate raising the issue of smoking and quitting, whilst engaging clients into a service.

It is useful to use open dialogue-driven 'starter for ten' questions, preferably ones which imply little or no personal involvement, such as 'What do you think about the smoke-free policy in pubs?'. This helps to establish a non-threatening, non-personal conversation about smoking without singling out the client to make a choice. It also helps to establish receptivity to messages of change. The aim is to have a conversation with the client about smoking to allow you to define whether to take the conversation further forward to contemplating ideas of stopping. When discussing smoking with a client, aim to use a reflective and flowing approach, so that you can make sure you know what is meant by the client. The client should talk more than you do in the intervention, so listen, then reflect it back, listen again and reflect again.

It is important to tell your client that you think they are doing well. Smokers often feel like they are 'social pariahs' and that society is judging them. Smoking is not validated as a bio-behavioural issue, but is often considered to be a social nuisance, which undermines the value and importance of the client stopping smoking. You can counter this by ensuring that they feel validated throughout the quit attempt. Fundamentally, the support you offer should involve you asking questions – trying not to give advice but to ask another question: 'I'm not sure, what do you think you could do about that?'. Aim to use the word 'could' (which implies choice), rather than 'should' (which implies an instruction): the sentences 'You could try eating raisins or grapes' or 'You should try eating raisins or grapes' have a very different impact on clients' perceptions of your support. Listen for a self-related statement from the client, especially if the client uses words like 'I' and 'me' to describe something. It has been suggested that, to impact upon change, these should fall into four general categories (Miller and Rollnick, 1991):

- Problem recognition – this is an issue
- Expression of concern – I am concerned about my smoking
- Intention to change – I would like to stop smoking
- Optimism about change – I think I could stop smoking

Exercise 3
Describe what happened when you have talked to someone about making a behaviour change and had a positive response. Did you use any of the tactics above?

Exercise 4: Time to reflect
What opportunities do you have for raising the issue of smoking in your practice?

Is it a standard part of your agenda – is it on your paperwork or system to automatically ask about smoking?

Why?

Is it always your clients' agenda to talk about their smoking?

What sort of things could you use to help the situation when you try to start a conversation about smoking (environment, relationship, how smoking is recorded, link to illness)?

What changes could you make to help smokers feel more at ease about talking about their smoking?

Practical?
1
2
3

Personal?
1
2
3

Client cue	Activity for facilitator
Not receptive to ideas about change	Reflect back what client has said Ask if client has any concerns about smoking. Build on their knowledge Provide written supportive information Offer choice of intervention
May be receptive	Provide information Why be a smoker? Why quit? Ask client to think about their normative social and personal smoking behaviour Offer choice and information about interventions
Receptive	Encourage support from smoking cessation service Specific, Measurable, Agreed, Realistic, Time-limited goal setting approach Client-centred and client-led approach
Changed recently	Encourage and offer praise Offer support and signpost to relapse prevention service
Relapse	Consider – was it a lapse or a relapse? Offer NRT/pharmacological support Offer support and signpost to relapse prevention service

Always try to use open and client-centred questions when discussing trying to stop smoking. Some starter questions might include the following:

- How do you feel about your smoking now compared to when you started?
- Has anything changed for you since you have been smoking in how you feel about it?
- If you wanted to stop smoking, do you think it would it be easy or difficult?
- How can I help?
- What do you think you will gain from stopping?
- What (or who) is stopping you from changing?
- Who would be helpful?
- Why have you come today?
- What do you think about... (topical local news item about smoking)

Figure 8 shows Prochaska and Diclemente's transtheoretical model of behavioural change.

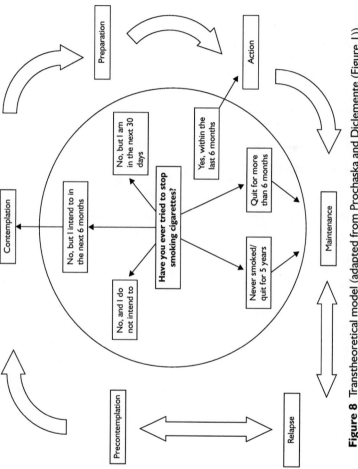

Figure 8 Transtheoretical model (adapted from Prochaska and Diclemente (Figure 1)).

Using neurolinguistic programming approaches

Neurolinguistic programming (NLP) consists of the use of repetitive or associative actions and language to support ideas and cues to behaviour. For example the use of words such as 'easy' or 'simply'. This can be supported by the addition of a repetitive behaviour. For example, every time the client thinks about the benefits of smoking they rub their hands and think about positive images.

An example of how language affects our feelings about power and the relationship between client and provider is the difference demonstrated below:

- I *need* <u>you</u> to stop smoking **for me**

or

- *If* **you** *would like* to stop smoking, I am here, and **you** can...

It can be used to focus goal-orientated services:

- What would **you** like to achieve?
- What would **you** like the outcome to be?

It can be used to support the client to define their own measures of success:

- How will **you** know you have achieved it?
- How can *I help?*

It can be used to help clients define their expectations and potential barriers to change:

- What happened last time?
- What do **you** think is stopping **you** currently?
- What has changed for **you**?
- What do **you** think might be hard to change?

It can be used to provide new replacement behaviours, such as using hand cream every time you want a cigarette, smelling the pleasant flavours and remembering the positive benefits.

A motivational approach

A motivational approach is one in which the client's perceptions of need and ability to change lead the intervention. The most commonly cited technique for a motivational approach is known as *motivational interviewing*. This has been defined as 'A directive, client centred counselling style for eliciting behaviour change by helping clients explore and resolve ambivalence' (Rollnick and Miller, 1995).

A motivational approach is one which is clearly:

- Focused on a clear outcome (in this case, stopping smoking)
- Goal orientated
- Subtle
- Based on an interpersonal relationship between client and facilitator

What do you need to be/do to deliver a motivational approach?

- Accept that the client knows their life best. That means that the client is the only person who can provide solutions.
- Listen for self-awareness and self-knowing statements.
- Monitor 'receptivity' to change.
- Support clients with the idea that they are able to make a choice – to smoke or not to smoke – and the role of the facilitator is to support informed choice and empowerment of clients to be able to perceive their ability to make a choice.

What is it not?

- Unsolicited, brief and opportunistic sign posting – sending someone to a service without their enthusiasm and support.

- Trying to persuade someone to try and stop smoking.
- A service which provides a one-size-fits-all solution.
- A teacher–pupil relationship between the expert facilitator and student client.
- A service which punishes those who cannot or do not chose to stop smoking.

Receptivity to change

There are three possible outcomes of any intervention or enquiry to a client about change – this can be a useful representation or analogy to help a client understand their position with regard to stopping smoking:

1. Not receptive to ideas of change – stopping smoking (the door is closed).
2. May be receptive to ideas of change – they might be aware of or thinking about stopping smoking (door is ajar).
3. Receptive to ideas of change – they are thinking and planning to stop (door is wide open).

These issues of receptivity are fluid and may be different with different facilitators. For example, a client may react differently to their mother suggesting change than to a professional.

The importance of understanding why people want to change

The reasons why people want to stop smoking are often referred to as *motivators*.

If the motivator is one that relates to changing for another person's gain, it is an external one. Good examples of external motivators are a pregnancy, instruction from a health professional, and pressure from the client's family and loved ones.

If the motivator is one that relates to the clients gain, it is an internal one. Good examples of internal motivators are the client explicitly stating that the client is changing for themselves, for a new car/house/holiday that the client wants (if it is for a new car/house/holiday for the family, and the rest of the family want it more than the client does, this is an external motivator), or to be able to take part in an activity enjoyed by the client (*to play football better* etc.). Human beings are intrinsically self-motivated because of our need to survive (our survival instinct), and this is what the internal/external motivator issue ably demonstrates. A useful question to translate this idea to a client is: *If you stop smoking, who will get the most out of it? Who will be the winner?*

If the client is demonstrating and talking about an external motivator to change their behaviour, the facilitator should facilitate the client in finding an internal motivator. For example:

Client: The kids really want me to stop smoking so that I can run around with them more, without getting out of breath.

Facilitator: How do you feel about that? Is it something you want to do?

Client: Well, I know they would like me to, so I should... but I'm not sure I want to run round with them. I'm exhausted most of the time anyway.

Facilitator: What can't you do now, that you would be able to do if you stopped smoking?

Client: Well, it would be nice to have some time for myself and maybe go swimming once a week with my friend Jenny. She goes to a lovely pool, but I haven't been because I can't afford it...

In this example, the facilitator has helped the client to see a personal reason for changing: that she would be able to go to the relaxing pool with her friend and have some time out from everyday stresses and strains – also potentially acting as a method of resolving her personal tension and stress.

Processes of quitting and supporting quit attempts – right time, right place, right service

As well as an internal motivator for change, the client also needs to feel that the time is right for them to attempt the behaviour change, and that they are personally prepared to try the change. The client's readiness to change can be assessed by asking, when the smoking problem is initially identified, whether they have ever attempted to change it before. For example:

Facilitator: You are a smoker?

Client: Yes, about 20 a day.

Facilitator: Have you ever tried to stop before?

The answers to this question are likely to be associated with or fall into one of six categories. The categories then relate to the stages of change identified by Prochaska and DiClemente (1983) in their 'transtheoretical model' (TTM) of behaviour change (Figure 8) and also referred to by Miller and Rollnick (1991) in their work about motivational interviewing. These responses can also be associated with the idea of a door – ajar, open or closed – as demonstrated in the analogy:

1. *No, and I don't want to stop now* or *I've stopped before but I don't want to stop now*. These clients are happy and comfortable in their behaviour and are known in the transtheoretical model as precontemplators. In terms of the doorway analogy, the door is shut.
2. *Yes I would like to stop in the next six months or so*. These clients are starting to consider making a change and are known in the transtheoretical model as *contemplators*. In relation to the doorway analogy, the door is ajar.

3. *Yes I would like to stop in the next month or so*. These clients are ready to make a change and are known in the transtheoretical model as *preparers*. In the doorway example, the door is open.

4. *Yes, I'm in the process now*. These clients are currently undergoing change and are considered to be in *action*, using the transtheoretical model. In the doorway model, the door is open, but it may, if there is a barrier or concern about progress, be starting to close.

5. *Yes, I've not long changed*. These clients are entering the phase of *maintenance*, if using the transtheoretical model, and are in a similar position to those described above with regard to the doorway analogy.

6. *I have made the change and maintained it for a considerable length of time*. These clients are securely in the maintenance phase of the transtheoretical model and are likely to stay not smoking, as long as they are supported to understand high-risk situations.

Precontemplators/door closed: happy in their behaviour

Most clients (around 60%) will be in this mindset when they are first approached and identified. People who are precontemplative will generally react in a very closed way to the idea of making a change. They may be *rebellious* to the idea, they may *rationalise* their current behaviour, they may be *resigned* to their current behaviour or they may be *reluctant* to consider the possibility of changing. In this case, it is very tempting to push clients into feeling guilty and making an attempt at behaviour change for the benefit of their health. In this circumstance, the client is likely to start lying to the facilitator about their behaviour, or to avoid the facilitator completely. The most appropriate and supportive action to take with a 'precontemplator' is to give them some written information leaflets to examine at their convenience (or to throw away!) and to have an open door policy: 'OK – it seems that now is not the best time for you to be thinking about stopping smoking, but have this leaflet and if you ever change your mind and feel that you have reached a point at which you would like to stop, come and see me any time... I have lots of ways that I can help you when the time is right.

Door ajar/contemplation: thinking about change as a possibility

Clients who are starting to consider change as a possibility are likely to be looking for information about their current and proposed behaviours and are likely to be analysing the personal risks involved in both changing and maintaining their current behaviour. They are often interested in factual information about their behaviour. The most appropriate action for these clients is to ask them to formalise the analytical process by considering something like a 'decisional balance' exercise (Health Education Authority, 1993). In this exercise, the client is asked to consider the positive and negative implications of maintaining and changing their behaviour. Table 1 shows a decisional balance for a chocolate eater.

The client then considers formally whether maintaining or changing the behaviour will give them increased positive outcomes, and if they are willing to consider the change.

A further strategy to support clients at this point would be to ask them to consider undertaking a written behavioural diary. This allows the client to see how the behaviour fits in with their current lifestyle and allows them to assess the strategies they may need to make a change. The diary should be kept over at least two days: one normal (e.g. working/school day) and one non-normal (e.g. weekend/day off etc.). Table 2 shows the categories

Table I Decisional balance exercise (adapted from Health Education Authority, 1993).

Positive implications of maintaining current behaviour (*eating chocolate*)	Negative implications of maintaining current behaviour (*eating chocolate*)
Personal pleasure chemicals *Taste enjoyment* *Personal treat/time* *Trigger for relaxation*	*None left for the rest of the family: family are irritated* *Costing money* *Makes me put on weight* *Reduces appetite for nutritionally improved food*
Positive implications of new behaviour (*not eating chocolate*)	**Negative implications of new behaviour (*not eating chocolate*)**
More appetite for nutritionally improved food *?Not putting on weight* *Family happier* *Increased money available*	*No personal trigger for relaxation* *No personal treat* *Lack of taste enjoyment*

Table 2 Example of categories in a smoking diary.

Time	Who with/ where	What did you do?	How felt before	How felt afterward	How much did you need to do the activity (1–5, 1 = not at all, 5 = desperate)?
10.00	Best friend at work	Smoked 2 cigs	Fed up of working	More relaxed	3

which need to be considered in a self-awareness diary. A useful reminder for the client relating to this is, whether they write it down or not (some clients do not want to formally record, or find it difficult to do so given their lifestyle), to consider for every cigarette smoked the following, based on the Rudyard Kipling poem:

> I knew six honest working men, they taught me all I knew,
> Their names were *what* and *why* and *when* and *how* and *where* and *who*.

Considering each of these six questions can help the client to become more self-aware about the normative values and triggers for smoking.

Door open/preparation: getting ready to make a change

The clients who are identified as very ready to make a change ('in preparation') could also be advised to complete the decisional balance and diary to help with planning the change. To be considered to be at this stage, the client needs to believe that the current behaviour is harmful, that their health/well being will be improved by making the change and that they have a good chance of succeeding if they make an attempt at the behaviour change.

Once the client is established as having an internal motivator, and to be ready to make an attempt at behaviour change, they need a supportive therapeutic plan to be negotiated together with the facilitator. In this, the facilitator should consider how often they would have contact with the client, how they will contact the client and what each contact is for. Clients need help to find their own solutions to their own issues; there is not a 'one-size-fits-all' prescription for behaviour change support. The facilitator should avoid being seen as the 'expert' in the client's behaviour change. The client should own the attempt and solutions to any issues that arise. For example, if a client is trying to maintain a change involving taking daily exercise, and they visit the facilitator and report that it is very difficult to do because the day seems to pass too quickly and there has been no time for the activity, the facilitator should ask the client to record a daily diary of what is happening throughout the day and then follow this by asking the client to consider where exercise might have been fitted in: picking the children up from school (could this have been done by walking; if not, could the client park away from the school and walk to it; could they take the stairs at work rather than the lift etc.)

Keeping the door open – 'action': changing the behaviour, and 'maintenance': keeping the change

Clients who are acting out a behaviour change or who have reached and are maintaining the new behaviour need help to avoid relapsing into the previous behaviour.

By assessing the clients' readiness and motivation to attempt a behaviour change, and tailoring their responses accordingly the facilitator will succeed in not alienating clients, and by supporting them, help them to choose their own life activities around smoking, underpinned by informed choice.

In order to be ready, willing and able to attempt to make a change like stopping smoking, the client needs to believe that:

1. The current smoking pattern has a negative consequence to the client, rather than to someone else (such as children, partners, the health service).
2. The negative consequence will be reduced or negated if they stop smoking, so it is worthwhile to make an attempt.
3. They have a good chance of succeeding if they try to change and stop smoking.

Understanding and demonstrating these ideals signifies a change in the client's decision-making process and mindset about smoking. It indicates

Exercise 5: The decisional balance for you

Fill in the decisional balance below, outlining the pros and cons using the previous part of the book to help you, of a change you would like to make for yourself.

The current situation/behaviour

PROS (Reasons for continuing current lifestyle)	CONS (Reasons for continuing current lifestyle)
PROS (Reasons for changing current lifestyle)	CONS (Reasons for changing current lifestyle)

Adapted from: Health Education Authority (1993).

If it is still difficult to distinguish the wood from the trees to see whether you would be better off changing, try scoring the pros and cons from 1–5 in terms of importance to you and totalling the result.

a level of confidence and also of more receptivity to the idea of trying to stop smoking, or making an attempt to stop smoking.

To support this effectively, the practitioner should try to:

■ Support and enhance the client's perceptions of confidence.
■ Remind the client of their stated reasons for wanting to stop smoking, returning to the things that the client thinks they will gain personally from stopping smoking – using the client's personal ideals of benefit to reinforce and support the client to keep goal-focused.
■ Support the client's increasing self-awareness, using self-awareness tools such as reflection on smoking and understanding triggers to smoke.

Exercise 6

This exercise can be useful for clients to supplement or replace an activity such as the decisional balance whilst achieving a similar understanding and self-awareness.

If you had to give a score out of ten to each of the items that you enjoy and dislike about smoking, what would the totals be at the bottom of each section?

What I feel I enjoy about smoking   **What I feel I dislike about smoking**

....
....
....
....
....

Totals ☐   ☐

- Help the client to identify options available to them – an abrupt quit attempt, supported cutting down, self-help, groups, one-to-ones etc.
- Provide information and access to other forms of support (such as medication, if this is appropriate and a choice they wish to make).

Pragmatic approaches to behaviour change

All human beings behave in certain ways to get their biological, sociological, behavioural and psychosocial needs met. Smoking may have fulfilled one or more of these roles in the client's life for some time, and it will be missed, and potentially reverted to for short- or long-term lapses. For example, Julie described visiting the pub after stopping smoking:

> There was a packet of cigarettes on the table and I felt really strange sitting there, with my drink in one hand and no cigarette in the other. I felt like my [smoking] hand was getting bigger and bigger, and I was so aware of it and uncomfortable that I went home early. It took a while before I could go out without feeling bad and like I was missing part of me.

For the behaviour change to be successful, suitable replacement activities and thoughts may need to be found by the client to meet the needs no longer satisfied by smoking. Julie talked about going home early, but that may not be something which could be sustained in the long term. Julie had to think of her own solution to the issue which would and could work for her.

Awareness of behaviours

Many of our behaviours are subconscious – we are not aware of them. You may have experienced driving somewhere and not being conscious of how you behaved at every roundabout, traffic light and junction – because for very experienced drivers, driving is subconscious behaviour.

It is important to assess knowledge, attitudes and behaviours both prior to and following personal or professional change for a number of reasons. Reflection on this experience is inherent to conscious experience of change and learning new behaviours.

Learning has been defined as 'the process of acquiring knowledge through experience which leads to a change in behaviour' (Jones, 1994). This suggests that learning for behaviour change is not simply theoretical, but applied in an experiential setting, increasing and enhancing confidence to change. Most competency-based learning is based on the Gestalt approach (Henrik, 1980) of five levels of competence:

1. Unconscious competence (not knowing you can do the new action)
2. Unconscious incompetence (not knowing you can't do the new action)
3. Conscious incompetence (knowing you can't do the new action)
4. Conscious competence (knowing you can do the new action)
5. Mastery (knowing you can do the new action, but it becoming instinctive and often subconscious).

This process is shown in Figure 9.

The use of knowledge, attitudes and behaviours as a function of change in competence is also based upon cognitive approaches to behavioural change which suggest that all three of these elements affect the individual's self-concept and self-belief. The cognitive approach is based upon the fundamental rationale that 'an individual's affect (mood, emotions) and behaviour are largely determined by the way in which he construes the world, that is how a person thinks determines how he feels and reacts' (Buchanan and Huczynski, 1985).

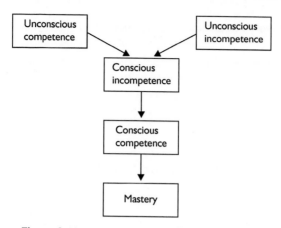

Figure 9 Unconscious and conscious competence.

Planning to change

When clients provide responses to cues which indicate that they are inter-ested in finding out more about stopping smoking, or would like to make a quit attempt, the facilitator should support the client to have a mental plan considering the:

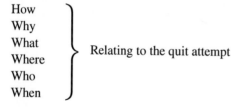

How
Why
What
Where
Who
When
} Relating to the quit attempt

Is the plan:

1. Specific
The plan needs to be clear and focused – **what** is the planned outcome?

2. Measurable
How will the client know they have achieved this? Is it tangible? Is it important to the client, or to someone else? **Why?**

3. Agreed between client, facilitator and other interested parties?

In making a plan to change behaviour such as smoking, the only person who can really make the plan work is the client themselves. Do they have support available at work, socially or from loved ones? **Who?** It is very important that stopping smoking is owned by the client and supported by those important to them. **What** support is available from you and others to help the client?

4. Realistic

Does the client believe it is achievable – **why**? **How** will they ensure that this continues?

5. Time-scale

When does the client feel they will have achieved a 'quit'? Do you agree?

Why do people smoke?

Starting smoking

Risk factors for starting to smoke include the following:

- Sociodemographic issues such as cultural and ethnic groupings, family structure, lower socio-economic status
- Environmental issues, such as having friends and family who are smoking, attachment patterns to people who smoke
- Behavioural issues such as educational and personal success, other risk behaviours, such as using other drugs, alcohol
- Personal issues such as depression, self-esteem, attitudes

People start to smoke ultimately because it is socially normal within their personal situation to do so and because they believe it provides a solution to an issue. This might include:

- Wanting to lose or maintain weight (especially for younger people)
- Wanting to fit in with a peer group – to be socially accepted
- Wanting to identify with being a smoker because it is trendy and because some celebrities smoke
- Media images support a cool and sexy image
- There is a perception it will relieve stress
- Marketing messages are subtle, often through brand identity and product placement

Maintaining smoking

People continue to smoke because they become biologically, behaviourally and psychosocially addicted to smoking. They begin to identify as 'a smoker'. An adult regular smoker is one who smokes every day.

Brand identity is important. Smokers are very brand loyal, and so will usually stick to a certain brand, because they prefer the taste of the recipe of one type of cigarette and because they like the brand association.

Although most cigarettes and tobacco contain the same plant-based tobacco, all of them taste different due to the many hundreds of additives. The additives allow the smoker to become more biologically addicted (some additives are there because of their addictive properties). Other additives allow the smoker to tolerate the nicotine better, making it smoother, more palatable and less nauseating – altogether manipulating the original plant product to maintain long-term smoking.

What is smoked tobacco?

Smoked tobacco, whether from manufactured cigarettes or from manufactured (roll your own – RYO) tobacco is derived, in the main from *Nicotiana tabacum* – athough nicotine, at some level, is present in a large number of *Nicotiana* plant species.

Levels of nicotine vary greatly between *Nicotiana* species and varieties. It is also affected to some extent by the processing methods used. However, it is the way that the cigarette is smoked which mostly affects the chemicals taken in by the smoker. Nicotine is addictive, with the chemical reaction caused by the effect of nicotine on the brain being the main cause – over time, the levels of chemical required to support normal 'pre-smoking' brain function is increased due to the chronic reaction in the brain to the chemicals absorbed by smoking tobacco.

Smoking is not purely about getting smoke into the lungs. Although many health promotion campaigns have focused so strongly on the lungs and respiratory system, smoked tobacco is essentially an effective method for delivering chemicals into the bloodstream, where they can be distributed around the body. Smoked tobacco provides a systemic effect, not a localised effect. It is a whole system chemical.

Tobacco smoke contains over 4,000 additives and chemicals, including at least 60 known carcinogens (according to the US Environmental Protection Agency). The chemicals include flavourings, including sugar and cocoa to counteract the emetic and bitter taste, smoothing chemicals to counteract the roughness of the chemical at a molecular level, and chemicals which enhance the addictive nature of tobacco.

Smoked tobacco may be obtained from manufactured cigars and cigarettes or from RYO or pipe tobacco. As a guide, one café crème-sized cigar is the chemical equivalent of 2–3 cigarettes, and one ounce of RYO is the chemical equivalent of 50 cigarettes.

Very quickly after breathing in the first puff of a cigarette (less than 10 seconds; see Figure 10), the chemicals are absorbed into the arterial system and nicotine is transferred across the blood–brain barrier. Count ten seconds out now – and then consider that if you had inhaled at the beginning of the count, when you finished the count chemicals would have

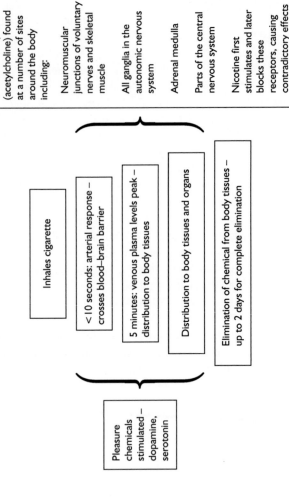

Figure 10 The effects of nictotine.

crossed into the brain. The chemicals prompt a specific set of neurons and in turn cause the brain to release noradrenaline and dopamine: 'pleasure chemicals'.

At the same time as this, while the cigarette is being finished (over a period of around five minutes) venous plasma levels peak, and the chemicals begin to be distributed widely around most of the body systems. Elimination of the chemicals then takes place, taking up to two days to eliminate totally the chemicals from one cigarette.

Smokers are able to maintain a fairly stable amount of chemicals in their blood by altering their smoking behaviour to maintain their preferred levels. Most smokers do not get up in the night to have a cigarette, because most regular (daily) smokers keep a high enough level of chemical in their blood through daily smoking. This, coupled with the slower rates of elimination, allows smokers some stability at night. Levels increase rapidly after the first cigarette of the day and are maintained at high levels by daytime smoking.

Smoked tobacco affects the brain by acutely increasing activity in the central reward pathway, delivering 'reward chemicals'. It also chronically reduces brain serotonin levels, potentially causing depression and low mood when quitting.

Psychological effects

There is no evidence that the biology of smoking reduces stress, although it does alleviate tobacco withdrawal symptoms which in themselves are stressful, both psychologically and physiologically.

The effects of smoking and stopping

Smoking and prescribed medication

Cigarette smoking involves the delivery of a set of drugs to most of the bodily organs. It causes the induction of the liver enzyme P450 1A2 (CYP1A2). When a smoker stops, this enzyme induction is lost, so there is slower metabolism of other drugs metabolised via the liver, leading to a rise in levels.

The most clinically significant drugs affected by cigarette smoking are clozapine and theophylline, both of which should be monitored during a quit attempt.

The acute effects of stopping smoking

The acute effects of stopping smoking last, in the main, for between one and 12 weeks. In the short term, clients may be surprised to note that they feel physically worse than they did whilst smoking. Around half to two-thirds of clients will experience mood swings, including irritability, aggression and depression. Sleep disturbance, restlessness and reduced levels of concentration affect a similar number of clients. It is well documented that, as confidence in the quit attempt increases in the client, anxiety reduces; therefore supporting the confidence of the client is a key element of the therapeutic intervention. Many smokers report increased coughing, throat soreness, chest problems and mouth ulcers. Unsurprisingly, in clients with greater cravings and more severe depression, relapse rates are higher.

Some other common tobacco withdrawal symptoms are:

- Lethargy
- Hunger and difficulty feeling full
- Decreased metabolism (basal metabolic rate and drugs)
- Increased cough
- Mouth ulcers
- Gastro-intestinal disturbance (often constipation)
- Strong cravings

To support clients with the acute effects of stopping smoking, the use of glucose or dextrose tablets, increased physical activity, relaxation techniques and reassurance of the temporary nature of withdrawal symptoms can all be used.

Prescription medications affected by smoking

Drug(s)	Interaction (effects compared with non-smokers)	Significance
Antipyrine Caffeine Desmethyldiazepam Estradiol Estrone Flecainide Heparin Imipramine Lidocaine Oxazepam Pentazocine Phenacetin Phenylbutazone Propranolol Theophylline	Accelerated metabolism	May require high doses in smokers, reduced doses after quitting
Oral contraceptives	Enhanced thrombosis, increased risk of stroke and myocardial infarction	Do not prescribe to smokers, especially if older than 35 years
Cimetidine and other H$_2$ blockers	Lower rate of ulcer healing, higher ulcer recurrence rates	Consider using mucosal protective agents
Propranolol	Reduced antihypertensive effect, reduced antianginal efficacy; greater effectiveness in reducing mortality following myocardial infarction	Consider the use of cardioselective beta-blockers
Nifedipine (and probably other calcium blockers)	Less anti-anginal effect	May require higher doses and/or multiple-drug anti-anginal therapy
Diazepam, chlordiazepoxide (and possibly other sedative-hypnotics)	Less sedation	Smokers may need higher doses
Chlorpromazine (and possibly other neuroleptics)	Less sedation, possibly reduced efficacy	Smokers may need higher doses
Propoxyphene	Reduced analgesia	Smokers may need higher doses

Pharmacological and other treatments

Smoking is a behaviour that has strong biological and psychological determinants: people smoke because of a physical addiction to nicotine, and because of a psychological addiction to the physical and social actions and rewards of smoking. Treatments available to smokers to help support a quit attempt need to take account of both the biological and behavioural triggers for smoking and need to provide alternatives and support to break both types of habit. All biological support to stop smoking should be supported by behavioural support either from group support or on a one-to-one basis. This vastly increases the likelihood of a successful quit attempt. Training courses to help nurses and other practitioners to support clients' quit attempts are widely available, or group or one-to-one support may be available through individual Primary Care Trust systems.

Behavioural support is centred on an assessment of the client's motivation and readiness to make an attempt at stopping smoking. The client needs to have an individual personal gain identified from stopping smoking, rather than being motivated by an external factor such as the children, future health or pressure from a health professional. They also need to be at a point where the attempt is a desired event by the smoker, and the client has optimism that they will be able to make a change.

Biological support centres on three types of pharmacological adjunct: nicotine replacement therapy (NRT), bupropion (Zyban) and varenicline (Chantix). NRT preparations, but not bupropion or varenicline, are listed in the *Nurse Prescribers' Formulary* and the *Nurse Prescribers' Extended Formulary*. The National Institute for Health and Clinical Effectiveness (2002) has recommended NRT or bupropion with behavioural support for smoking cessation (although NRT and bupropion should not be used together). Varenicline has yet to be approved as it only entered the market in late 2006.

NRT replaces the nicotine that smokers are used to receiving from cigarettes in a gradually reducing dose over a period of 8–12 weeks. Often clients will want to reduce this time period: this is not advisable, as they are at higher risk of relapse (starting smoking again) if they do not take the full treatment course (National Institute for Health and Clinical Effectiveness, 2002). NRT is available in a number of delivery systems (chewing gum, lozenge, 24-hour patch, 16-hour patch, inhalator, nasal spray and sublingual microtab). The type of delivery mechanism should ideally be chosen by the client to suit his or her lifestyle: gum may not be suitable for someone who works over the counter in a bank, for example. There are three different brands of NRT patch (2 × 24 hour and 1 × 16 hour) which all work in different ways, so clients should not be advised to switch between different brands of patch. However, if a patch disagrees with them, they may wish to try a different type of NRT such as gum or lozenge. There is currently no evidence that any one particular type of NRT delivery system works better or worse than another (British Medical Journal, 2001), although higher dose gum is more effective than lower dose gum in dependent smokers, underlining the fact that the choice of delivery system relates mostly to the client's lifestyle.

The *nasal spray* is very fast acting and mimics the plasma profile of cigarettes. It is very useful for heavily dependent smokers, but can cause throat irritation, sneezing, watering eyes and allergic reactions. It is cautioned in clients with peptic ulcer and chronic nasal disorders. One dose = 1 spray in each nostril, 1–2 doses per hour, no more than 3 doses per hour. The maximum dose is 32 doses in 24 hours.

Microtabs and *lozenges* are useful for light to moderate smokers or those reducing from something higher strength. They should be avoided in people with peptic ulcers. They are fast acting, discreet and give good control. The dosage is 1–2 per hour (microtabs are sublingual); average daily doses are around 8–12, with maximum doses 40 daily (microtabs) and 25 daily (lozenges). Acidic drinks should be avoided for 15 minutes prior to consuming lozenges.

Chewing gum is fast acting and gives good control and oral stimulation. It is available in two strengths: 2 mg for light/moderate smokers (less than 20 per day) and 4 mg for heavier smokers (more than 20 per day). Again, they should be avoided in clients with histories of peptic ulcers, gastritis, oesophagitis and pharyngitis. It can cause increased salivation, hiccups and mouth or throat irritation. Acidic drinks should be avoided for 15 minutes prior to consuming gum. One piece per hour is the average dosage (12–15 per day). The full dosage should be taken for 12 weeks, than tapered off to 1–2 pieces per day. Treatment is not recommended beyond 12 months.

The *inhalator* is fast-acting and provides hand to mouth activity (although this can continue a psychological habit). It should be avoided in those with peptic ulcers, and is useful for those who are finding the rituals of smoking difficult to conquer. The dosage is 6–12 cartridges daily; then after 6–8 weeks the dosage should be gradually reduced. Treatment should not continue past 6 months.

Sixteen-hour patches are relatively slow acting (around 20 minutes), but aim to mimic daily smoking patterns and plasma profiles. It is also discreet and suitable for those who smoke regularly through the day. Clients should be advised never to start on the lowest strength, but should use the high-strength patch for 8 weeks, mid-strength for 2 weeks, and low strength for 2 weeks. It should be applied to a clean, dry, intact, hairless area of skin on the hip, chest or upper arm, using a different area each day.

Twenty-four hour patches are relatively slow acting (around 20 minutes), and are suitable for clients who prefer the confidence of knowing they have 24-hour cover, or those who feel that they are most addicted. They are discreet. Clients with chronic skin conditions should avoid it. In those who smoke more than 20 per day (or have chemical results which suggest this – heavy smokers) the dosage is high-strength patch for 3–4 weeks, mid-strength patch for 3–4 weeks, and then low strength patch for 3–4 weeks. In those who smoke less than 20 per day, the dosage is mid-strength for 3–4 weeks, low strength for 3–4 weeks.

All patches can cause itching and erythema, and clients with chronic skin conditions should avoid their use.

Any form of NRT is commonly contraindicated in patients who have/had:

- Acute myocardial infarction
- Unstable angina
- Severe cardiac arrhythmia
- Recent cerebrovascular accident

(Sources of information taken from manufacturers' data sheets and monographs: Pharmacia Ltd, GlaxoSmithKline and Novartis Consumer Healthcare.)

NRT may be given to adolescents under medical advice if they are smoking more than 10 cigarettes per day. Similarly, pregnant and lactating women should be advised to attempt to quit without NRT, but if this proves impossible, a risk assessment should be undertaken and NRT prescribed where necessary, again under medical advice (National Institute of Clinical Effectiveness, 2002; http://www.givingupsmoking.co.uk/). The risk of becoming addicted (dependent) on NRT is small. About 1 in 20 people who stop smoking with the help of NRT continue to use NRT in the longer term.

The other commonly used NICE-approved adjunct to smoking cessation is bupropion, commonly known as Zyban. Bupropion is not suitable for those under 18 as its efficacy has not been tested, and is not suitable for pregnant women (National Institute of Clinical Effectiveness, 2002).

This drug works on the brain, and it is thought to reduce the physiological rewards received from smoking. It works for some patients but not for all, and it is not possible to tell for whom it will be effective until they have tried it. It was originally developed in the USA as an antidepressant, and was found to have a pronounced effect upon smoking rates. It is not licensed in the UK as an antidepressant. It is only to be used, under the terms of licensing, if it is supported by behavioural change support. It is contraindicated in the following groups:

- Has a current seizure disorder or any history of seizures.
- Has a current or previous diagnosis of bulimia or anorexia nervosa.
- Has a known central nervous system tumour.
- Is experiencing abrupt withdrawal from alcohol or benzodiazepines.
- Hypersensitivity to bupropion or any of the excipients.
- Severe hepatic cirrhosis.
- History of bipolar disorder.
- Concomitant use with monoamine oxidase inhibitors (MAOI).
- It is not recommended in pregnancy or lactation.

It takes around a week to build up effective blood levels, so a course of bupropion should be started at least 7 days prior to the quit date. The recommended dosage of bupropion is 150 mg once per day (one tablet) for the first six days, then 300 mg (two tablets) daily thereafter. A full treatment course lasts 7–9 weeks and clients should be encouraged to complete the full course to maximise their chances of success. The risk of seizure on this dosage is classed as rare (0.1%), but this risk increases if the dosage is increased. Discontinuation reactions are not expected due to the long half-life of the drug, so it is not necessary to taper off the dosage (GlaxoSmithKline, 2001). Bupropion is a black-triangle drug, and is therefore subject to intense scrutiny of adverse reactions by the Committee for the Safety of Medicines (CSM). Clinical trials show 60% of clients quit at 4 weeks and 28% quit at 12 months.

Bupropion is not listed in the *Nurse Prescribers' Formulary* or the *Nurse Prescribers' Extended Formulary*. This means that although nurses and clients may feel that bupropion is the most suitable pharmacological support for the client's lifestyle, nurses may need to have a standard letter explaining this which they can forward to the GP or other medical prescriber.

Bupropion works for some people but not for all, and as the exact way in which the drug works is currently unknown, there is no effective method for testing clients to identify those for whom it would work best.

Varenicline is a new drug and does not yet have NICE approval, although it should have some time this year. It is a prescription-only medication and should be used in the same way as Bupropion and NRT, as an adjunct to stopping smoking. In clinical trials it was found to be very effective, in conjunction with behavioural support, in supporting long-term abstinence from smoking. Varenicline can bind to some of the nicotinic receptors – the a4ß2 acetylcholine receptors. When binding to these receptors, varenicline acts in two ways: it acts like nicotine (partial agonist), helping to relieve craving symptoms, but it also acts against nicotine (antagonist) by taking its place, helping to reduce the pleasurable effects of smoking. The most common side-effects (seen in more than 1 patient in 10) are nausea, insomnia (difficulty sleeping), abnormal dreams and headache.

Patients should first set a date when they will stop. Then they begin treatment 1 to 2 weeks before that date. Treatment starts with one 0.5 mg tablet daily for 3 days, followed by a further 4 days during which the patient takes one 0.5 mg tablet twice daily. A starter pack is available on initiation of the drug regime. From then on, the patient takes one 1 mg tablet twice daily until the end of treatment (12 weeks). The dose may be reduced to 0.5 mg twice a day in patients who do not tolerate the 1 mg twice daily dose. At the end of the 12 weeks, in patients who have stopped smoking, doctors may choose to carry on treatment for another 12 weeks.

There is rarely one perfect pharmacological adjunct in smoking cessation. For most people, there will be several suitable treatments, possibly including more than one type of NRT or (assuming no contraindication) bupropion. Therefore, the nurse or facilitator's role in supporting and using pharmacological adjuncts to facilitate change is to identify the most suitable therapies, describe the positives and negatives related to those treatments to the individual and allow them to make a personal and informed choice. In this way, clients are more likely to be compliant with therapy and are more likely to have ownership of the change attempt.

Giving clients the right pharmacological information, and their use of these adjuncts with behavioural support, is likely to increase their chance of success in stopping smoking and making their future healthier and wealthier.

Current NRT products for prescribing

NRT product	Amount to supply
Boots Patch 21 mg	Box of 7
Boots Patch 14 mg	Box of 7
Boots Patch 7 mg	Box of 7
Nicorette Patch 15 mg	Box of 7
Nicorette Patch 10 mg	Box of 7
Nicorette Patch 5 mg	Box of 7
Nicotinell Patch 21 mg	Box of 7
Nicotinell Patch 14 mg	Box of 7
Nicotinell Patch 7 mg	Box of 7
Nic CQ Patch 21 mg	Box of 7
Nic CQ Patch 14 mg	Box of 7
Nic CQ Patch 7 mg	Box of 7
Nic CQ Gum 2 mg	12 Pack
Nic CQ Gum 2 mg	96 Pack
Nic CQ Gum 4 mg	12 Pack
Nic CQ Gum 4 mg	24 Pack
Nic CQ Gum 4 mg	96 Pack
Nicorette Gum 2 mg	105 Pack
Nicorette Gum 2 mg	15 Pack
Nicorette Gum 2 mg	30 Pack
Nicorette Gum 4 mg	105 Pack
Nicorette Gum 4 mg	15 Pack
Nicorette Gum 4 mg	30 Pack
Nicotinell Gum 2 mg	12 Pack
Nicotinell Gum 2 mg	24 Pack
Nicotinell Gum 2 mg	96 Pack

NRT product	Amount to supply
Nicotinell Gum 4 mg	12 Pack
Nicotinell Gum 4 mg	24 Pack
Nicotinell Gum 4 mg	96 Pack
Nicotinell Lozenges 1 mg	12 Pack
Nicotinell Lozenges 1 mg	36 Pack
Nicotinell Lozenges 1 mg	96 Pack
Nic CQ Lozenges 2 mg	36 Pack
Nic CQ Lozenges 2 mg	72 Pack
Nic CQ Lozenges 4 mg	36 Pack
Nic CQ Lozenges 4 mg	72 Pack
Nicorette Inhalator Refill Pack	42 Cartridges
Nicorette Inhalator Starter Pack	6 Cartridges
Nicorette Microtabs	105 Pack
Nicorette Nasal Spray	1 bottle/10 ml

Cut down to quit

It is well documented that cutting down is often counter-productive as clients feel they should be rewarded for their change in behaviour, but the health professional is often aware of the lack of positive health effect of this change and feels compromised by wanting to provide positive feedback while simultaneously informing the client of the fact.

Regular smokers are able to self-titrate their nicotine intake by the use of compensatory smoking mechanisms. They are self-medicating nicotine addicts who need a particular individual dose of plasma nicotine to be delivered through their cigarette use. This means, in effect, that they will alter their smoking behaviours (drawing deeper, longer, more draws per cigarette etc.) to access the nicotine their body requires to function without withdrawal and physical, emotional and psychological negative consequences.

Therefore, 'cutting down' has never been the appropriate mechanism for clients wanting to stop smoking. A new product licence for two existing forms of nicotine replacement therapy – the inhalator and freshmint gum from Nicorette – allows a recommendation to be made to some clients for cutting down to achieve complete abstinence. In summary, the client is advised to cut down their cigarette consumption over a period of weeks, whilst simultaneously slowly increasing their use of the nicotine replacement therapy to provide the background venous plasma nicotine required by the addicted smoker, preventing them from altering their smoking behaviour to receive the necessary amount of nicotine from the cigarette. The client may be asked to self-fund this period of NRT prior to achieving the quit date to provide an element of self-commitment from the smoker to the quit attempt. At quit date, they may be able to join an NHS scheme which will often provide post-quit NRT as well as behavioural support.

The evidence suggests that clients are more likely to be quit at 12 months if they reach half consumption at six weeks following starting the course. The protocol shown in Figure 11 is a suggestion for how the programme may be used.

This is not a replacement for abrupt cessation attempts, but is an alternative option for those who feel they would like to quit but who feel that an

Dear

Congratulations on wanting to stop smoking. You have chosen to cut down cigarettes at the same time as supporting yourself with Nicotine Replacement Therapy (NRT). You can use this method to help you get to a particular date when you plan to stop smoking. Your planned date for stopping smoking is 1 February 2006. This gives you 12 weeks to achieve 0 cigarettes per day. You have chosen to use the inhalator. You are currently smoking 40 cigarettes per day.

If possible, please can you sign below so that we are able to contact you and find out how you get on?

Client name: Bob Jones

Week commencing	Number cigarettes per day	Number of pieces of gum/cartridges per day	Date achieved	Notes
7 November	37	1	7 November	Happy, no problems
14 November	34	2	14 November	No problems
21 November	30	3	20 November	No problems
28 November	27	4	28 November	Hard week but made it!
5 December	24	5	5 December	No problems, back on track
12 December	20	6	11 December	Half way!!!
19 December	17	7		
26 December	14	8		
3 January	10	9		SEE PRACTICE FACILITATOR FOR CO READ
10 January	7	10		
17 January	4	11		
24 January	0	12		JOIN LOCAL NHS SCHEME

CO reading at point of starting cut down: 48
Date reached cigarette abstinence:
Joined NHS: Y/N
Date joined LSSS:
Still quit at 4 weeks post abstained?

Figure 11 Example protocol.

abrupt attempt is not for them at this moment. In the past this group have generally been advised to continue their smoking and contemplate changing at a later date. In every 100,000 adults, approximately 25,000 will be regular smokers. Around half of these are not ready to consider quitting, 3–4,000 will consider an abrupt attempt and around 8–9,000 are unsure of their position and would theoretically like to stop, but do not feel that this is their time for an abrupt attempt. This group may be recruited to stop smoking through this new mechanism. This is a group not currently offered any appropriate intervention and the evidence suggests that the 12 month quit rate is similar to that in clients offered abrupt cessation methods.

The importance of the new indication lies in the increased choice which can be offered to smokers to help them stop smoking. This indication also reinforces the importance of identifying smokers who may consider quitting over a longer period, as opposed to those who are ready, willing and able to make an abrupt quit attempt.

NRT technique and dosage

Information in the table on the following pages is taken from manufacturers' data sheets and monographs.

Product	Technique	Dosage
Nasal spray	Prime the spray before first use or if not used for 2–3 days: press the shoulders of the spray device up to 7 or 8 times until a fine spray appears Keeping the head level, gently tilt the spray and insert the nozzle into the nostril. Press the shoulders of the bottle to activate the spray	One dose = 1 spray into each nostril 1–2 doses per hour, no more than 3 doses per hour Maximum dose: 64 sprays (32 doses) in 24 hours Treat for 3 months before weaning off for 6–8 weeks Treatment beyond 6 months not recommended
Microtabs	Place the tablet under the tongue and allow to dissolve slowly. Do not chew or swallow. Avoid acidic drinks for 15 minutes before use	1 tablet per hour if less dependent (less than 20/day) 2 tablets per hour if more dependent (more than 20/day) Average daily dose: 8–12 tablets (low dependence) 16–24 tablets (high dependence) Absolute maximum: 40 tablets daily Full dosage for 3 months then gradually reduce the dosage. Stop when using 1–2 tablets per day. Treatment beyond 12 months not recommended
Lozenges	Suck one lozenge until the taste becomes strong Park the lozenge between the gum and cheek. When the taste fades, suck the lozenge again. Repeat until the lozenge has dissolved completely (about 30 minutes) Avoid acidic drinks for 15 minutes before use	One lozenge every 1–2 hours Average daily dose: 8–12 lozenges Absolute maximum: 25 lozenges Full dosage for 3 months then gradually reduce the dosage. Stop when reduced to 1–2 lozenges per day. Treatment beyond 6 months not recommended.

Product	Technique	Dosage
Gum	Start chewing slowly – around 15 chews are needed for initial release of nicotine	2 mg gum if less dependent (less than 20/day)
	When you feel a tingling sensation or when the taste becomes strong park the gum between the cheek and teeth	4 mg gum if more dependent (more than 20/day)
		Initially use an average of one piece of gum per waking hour (12–15 pieces per day)
	When tingling or taste has almost gone start chewing again	Full dosage for 3 months the gradually taper off. Stop when down to 1–2 pieces per day. Treatment beyond 12 months not recommended.
	Chew each piece of gum for 20–30 minutes	
	Avoid acidic drinks for 15 minutes before and during chewing	Cut down to stop
		Replace gradually cigarettes with NRT, aiming for at least half cigarette consumption by 6 weeks. Treatment beyond 12 months not recommended
Inhalator	Pull the two parts of the mouthpiece apart, insert a cartridge and reassemble the mouthpiece. This breaks the seals on the cartridge	6–12 cartridges daily to start
		Reduce daily dosage gradually over 6–8 weeks
		Treatment beyond 6 months not recommended
	Inhale through the mouthpiece – shallow puffing or deep inhalations are equally effective	Cut down to stop
	The number, frequency and duration of inhalations will depend on the individual and their previous smoking habit	Replace gradually cigarettes with NRT, aiming for at least half cigarette consumption by 6 weeks. Treatment beyond 12 months not recommended

Product	Technique	Dosage
16 hour patches	Apply to clean, dry, intact areas of hairless skin on the hip, chest or upper arm.	Never start on the lowest strength
		Do not cut in half
	Use a different site every day	High-strength patch for 8 weeks
	Reapply a new patch every day (usually in the morning)	Mid-strength patch for 2 weeks
	Remove the patch at night after approx. 16 hours wear	Low-strength patch for 2 weeks
	Dispose of patch by folding in half with the gummed edges innermost and wrap in the original foil pack or a piece of kitchen foil.	Review after three months and consider a further treatment period if abstinence not achieved, but motivation is still strong.
		Treatment over 12 months not recommended
24 hour patches	Remove metal backing, put on the skin and hold in place with the palm of the hand for 10–20 seconds	Do not cut in half
		High dependence (more than 20/day)
	Apply to clean, dry, intact areas of hairless skin on the hip, chest or upper arm.	High-strength patch for 3–4 weeks
		Mid-strength patch for 3–4 weeks
	Use a different site every day	Low-strength patch for 3–4 weeks
	Reapply a new patch every day	Low dependence (less than 20/day)
	Dispose of patch by folding in half with the gummed edges in-nermost and wrap in the original foil pack or a piece of kitchen foil.	Mid-strength patch for 3–4 weeks
		Low-strength patch for 3–4 weeks
		Review after three months and consider a further treatment period if abstinence not achieved but motivation is still strong
		Treatment over 12 months not recommended

Relapse prevention

Stopping smoking remains the single most important thing that people can do to improve their health and social outcomes. However, more than 80% of the people who try to quit smoking relapse or return to smoking within a year, with the majority relapsing within a week. Most smokers take several attempts to stop, showing that many experience one or more episodes of relapse before they are able to become long-term non-smokers. For practitioners this can be at best frustrating and at worst demoralising and disempowering, as we are often unsure of how to help.

In terms of relapse prevention, little evidence is available to support current practice. A recent Cochrane review (Hajek *et al.*, 2005) suggested that there is currently insufficient evidence to support the use of any specific intervention for helping smokers who have successfully stopped smoking cigarettes for a short time to avoid longer term relapse. They concluded that the evidence was strongest for interventions focusing on identifying and resolving tempting situations, simply because most of the studies reviewed were concerned with this.

Relapse often occurs because clients find themselves smoking in response to a situation in which they would normally smoke. After a period of 1–2 weeks this is rarely due to a biological urge or desire to smoke to provide the chemical relief from withdrawal symptoms, but is more often an emotional response to a situation. Clients need to be aware of their triggers in these situations and to have considered the possibility of these situations occurring so that they can plan a strategy to help them avoid smoking.

Relapse is not always inevitable, but it is part of the process of change, particularly when people try to make major changes in addictive behaviours. Even more common are temporary returns to smoking, known as *lapses*.

In the Prochaska and DiClemente model of change, relapse is seen as an integral part of the change process. However, several criticisms of this model for the sustained achievement of change have been put forward. In practice, when we try to change behaviour we often learn a considerable amount through our own past mistakes. We identify which situations are high risk for us and which strategies either do or do not help us cope. We also learn how to prevent a single episode of the old behaviour from turning into a 'relapse' – a complete return to former patterns and lifestyles.

Following a brief intervention, there are three possible outcomes of any intervention or enquiry to a client about change:

1. Not receptive to ideas of change (the door is closed)
2. May be receptive to ideas of change (door is ajar)
3. Receptive to ideas of change (door is wide open)

These issues of receptivity are fluid and may be different with different facilitators. For example, a client may react differently to their mother suggesting change than to a professional.

High risk situations

Eighty per cent of people who make a quit attempt relapse within the first 12 months – that is, they return to smoking at a similar level to that which they were doing before the quit attempt. Peters (1983) suggested several identifying factors which indicate increased risk of relapse:

- inadequate skills to deal with social pressure to use substances
- frequent exposure to 'high-risk situations' that have led to use in the past
- physical or psychological reminders of use (e.g. smoking paraphernalia, smoking friends, money)
- inadequate skills to deal with interpersonal conflict or negative emotions
- desires to test personal control over tobacco
- recurrent thoughts or physical desires to use tobacco

These are areas to ask clients about so that they are able to think about these issues in advance.

You could use a checklist like this:

- Establish and acknowledge the client's feelings about the lapse
- Check: is it a slip or full relapse?
- Reflect on previous experience – what happened and why?

- Identify better coping strategies for high-risk situations – what could they have done differently instead of having the cigarette?
- Check receptivity is still present
- Reassess biological needs
- Offer an anchor to a new behaviour instead of a cigarette (associate with positive emotions), such as deep breathing or pleasant smell from hand cream.

Monitoring and evaluation

The Department of Health states that all advisors providing smoking cessation support *must*:

- Have received appropriate training (see competencies in previous section).
- Carry out four-week follow-up promptly (this means that all smokers making a quit attempt should be contacted by the advisor four weeks after the date of their planned quit attempt to check their smoking status).
- Complete the minimum data set (individual client monitoring forms) for each client and return the data to the smoking cessation coordinator at the PCT or organisation.
- Offer weekly support for at least the first four weeks of a quit attempt (this could be by telephone, email or face-to-face contact)
- Attempt to confirm smoking status using a CO monitor, wherever possible, and record the outcome.

The information gathered by advisors/facilitators through monitoring forms informs the Department of Health of the success or failure or smoking cessation services, and allows decisions to be made regarding the continuation or otherwise of funding for such services.

The following is an example of a monitoring form. This should be completed by the facilitator and sent to the local service provider for data entry.

SMOKING CESSATION 4 WEEKS		
ATTENDANCE DATE:		
MONITORING FORM		
CLINIC NAME:	ADVISOR:	
CLIENT DETAILS		
FORENAME:	SURNAME:	
ADDRESS:	SEX:	
	ETHNICITY (please circle)	
	WHITE	MIXED
TOWN:	ASIAN	BLACK
COUNTY:	OTHER	UNKNOWN
POSTCODE:	D.O.B:	
TEL:	AGE:	
PREGNANT: YES/NO		
ENTITLED TO FREE PRESCRIPTIONS?: YES/NO		
FREE PRESCRIPTION CLASSIFICATION:		
CLIENT RECEIVED NRT?: YES/NO		
Medication received (notes and dates)		
CLIENT RECEIVED BUPROPION (ZYBAN): YES/NO		
CLIENT RECEIVED VARENICLINE (CHANTIX): YES/NO		
AGREED QUIT DATE:	**ACTUAL QUIT (IF APPLICABLE) DATE:**	
4 WEEK FOLLOW-UP		
EXPECTED DATE OF FOLLOW-UP:		
LOST TO FOLLOW-UP?		
CONTACT METHOD: PHONE/LETTER/FACE-TO-FACE		
CONTACT DATE:		
DATE OF LAST SMOKE:		
STILL SMOKING: YES/NO		
CO TEST DONE: YES/NO		
CO LEVEL:	CO CONFIRM NOT SMOKING: YES/NO	
AUTHORISATION		
This form will be stored on the organisation computer for monitoring purposes only. It is in the interest of research into good practice, etc. This is my agreement...................................Date................................		

The six categories of intervention

Consider the type of service you currently provide. Which of these categories does it fit into? What can you change about your practice to move forward?

Prescription **Give advice** – be judgmental, critical or evaluative. A prescriptive intervention is one that explicitly seeks to direct the behaviour of the patient especially, though not exclusively, outside the consultation. 'Go to bed for a week' or 'Take these tablets four times a day'.	Information **Inform** – be didactic, instruct, or interpret. An informative intervention endeavours to give new knowledge to the patient. 'You have pneumonia'; 'Your ECG was normal'.
Confrontation **Give feedback** – be challenging, give direct feedback. A confronting intervention directly challenges the attitudes, behaviour or belief of the patient. 'I can see you find it difficult to talk about your mother's death'; 'You don't seem to hear what I am saying to you'; 'Have you taken your tablets regularly?'	Support Is approving, validating, confirming, appreciating. A supportive intervention affirms the worth and value of the patient. 'I understand'; 'You have had a tough time'; 'You seem to have coped extremely well'; or a nod of the head, supportive grunts etc.
Catharsis Encourages and allows the release of laughter, tears, anger or fear. A cathartic intervention tries to help the release of painful emotion or tensions. It can be words, 'You are obviously distressed'; 'I can see that you are tearful about this'; or bodily response such as an arm around the shoulder.	Catalysis Encourages the patient to talk about what worries him; it does not direct and is not judgmental. A catalytic intervention is enabling; it encourages self-direction and allows the patient to go the way he wishes to. An open-ended manoeuvre is simply reflecting back to the patient key words, his last word or phrase or non-verbal signs.

Heron (1990)

Which level do you practise at?

Competence exercise

Now you are at the end of the book, consider your competence levels. As at the beginning of the book, read each of the following statements and rate your current ability/competence to undertake the competency. Ratings are 1–5 (1 being novice) to 5 (being expert). These are adapted from the competencies required by the UK Department of Health for facilitators of smoking cessation.

Example

Brief interventions

Competency	Rating and thoughts
Ask about smoking in an appropriate way to elicit an accurate response	4: I would ask in a subtle way – trying to be non threatening and non judgemental
Record status and action taken in an appropriate system	4: I will use a monitoring form and keep in a folder
Assess readiness to quit and willingness to use appropriate treatments	4: I can use the verbal and non-verbal cues provided by clients to identify their receptivity and interest
Understanding and dissemination of the health risks of smoking and the benefits of quitting	4: I am clear that smoking tobacco is a systemic issue and that stopping smoking is the single best thing someone can do to improve their health outcomes
Understanding and describing the reasons why stopping smoking can be difficult	4: I understand that it is difficult to stop because of the sociology, psychology and biology of smoking
Know what treatments are available to help with stopping smoking	4: I understand that there are services which support both biology, sociology and psychology of stopping smoking
Know how to refer to local services	1: I will contact my local healthcare provider to find out more
Understanding of the wider context of smoking cessation	4: I understand that smoking tobacco affects people across the world, and that smoking cessation is an important international public health issue

One-to-one support and advice

Competency	Rating and thoughts
Understand and describe national patterns of smoking behaviour as a function of age, gender, ethnic origin and social class	3: I understand the risk factors for smoking and that inequalities and vulnerability increases the risk of regular smoking
Understand and describe behavioural and pharmacological determinants of smoking behaviour (including perceived benefits and disbenefits of smoking and quitting)	4: I am able to identify and support clients who are receptive, using behavioural and biological support mechanisms
Understand and demonstrate awareness of smoking cessation treatment methods, their effectiveness, appropriateness and evaluation	4: I can support clients with counselling interventions, and can offer them advice re pharmacology too, giving them an increased chance of stopping. I can monitor the outcomes using the monitoring tool
Demonstrate the ability to assess a client	4: I can assess the client by taking account of dependence on smoking, commitment to quit, past quit/smoking history, and can use CO monitors as a motivational, assessment and validatory tool
Understand and be able to describe pharmacotherapy available to aid smoking cessation and demonstrate the ability to help clients choose the most appropriate supporting pharmacotherapy for each client	4: I can describe and discuss the use of NRT and or Zyban as an adjunct to stopping smoking
Be able to offer appropriate, timely behavioural support	4: I can offer support without a waiting list, and can offer relapse prevention too
Describe and plan appropriate treatment plans, aim, length, method and benefits	3: I can describe and offer clients support over a time period which suits them, looking to use a disengagement plan – so that they take ownership of the stop smoking attempt
Describe and plan monitoring	4: I will follow my clients up 4 weeks post-quit, 3 months post-quit and 12 months post-quit

Group interventions

Competency	Rating and thoughts
Describe potential difficulties in recruiting clients, and methods for dealing with these	4: Not all clients want to go to groups – some people will offer cues which suggest they would rather have a one-to-one. Marketing may be needed
Demonstrate the ability to assess suitability for group treatment	4: Clients with a high social need for smoking and who would benefit from peer support
Demonstrate awareness of the logistics of running groups	4: A group needs a group plan, with an identified plan – number of sessions, breaks, activities to be attractive to clients
Plan and describe a treatment programme for groups	4: See plan
Demonstrate awareness of group processes and how they can help or hinder motivation to quit within the group	4: Group dynamics affect the group – it is important to act as facilitator not teacher and to keep the group flowing
Demonstrate awareness and strategies for dealing with 'problem' group members	4: An open and honest demeanour will help – talking to clients and asking if they are finding the group useful
Plan and evaluate a method of keeping records of group attendance and outcome	4: I will use the monitoring tool during the group times, and will follow people up by phone or email afterwards
Show awareness of maintenance/relapse support systems	4: I will offer drop-in groups twice a year for relapse prevention and will invite all of my clients

Brief interventions

Competency	Rating and thoughts
Ask about smoking in an appropriate way to elicit an accurate response	
Record status and action taken in an appropriate system	
Assess readiness to quit and willingness to use appropriate treatments	
Understanding and dissemination of the health risks of smoking and the benefits of quitting	
Understanding and describing the reasons why stopping smoking can be difficult	

Know what treatments are available to help with stopping smoking	
Know how to refer to local services	
Understanding of the wider context of smoking cessation	

One-to-one support and advice

Competency	Rating and thoughts
Understand and describe national patterns of smoking behaviour as a function of age, gender, ethnic origin and social class	
Understand and describe behavioural and pharmacological determinants of smoking behaviour (including perceived benefits and disbenefits of smoking and quitting)	
Understand and demonstrate awareness of smoking cessation treatment methods, their effectiveness, appropriateness and evaluation	
Demonstrate the ability to assess a client	
Understand and be able to describe pharmacotherapy available to aid smoking cessation and demonstrate the ability to help clients choose the most appropriate supporting pharmacotherapy for each client	
Be able to offer appropriate, timely behavioural support	
Describe and plan appropriate treatment plans, aim, length, method and benefits	
Describe and plan monitoring	

Group interventions

Competency	Rating and thoughts
Describe potential difficulties in recruiting clients, and methods for dealing with these	
Demonstrate the ability to assess suitability for group treatment	
Demonstrate awareness of the logistics of running groups	
Plan and describe a treatment programme for groups	
Demonstrate awareness of group processes and how they can help or hinder motivation to quit within the group	
Demonstrate awareness and strategies for dealing with 'problem' group members	
Plan and evaluate a method of keeping records of group attendance and outcome	
Show awareness of maintenance/relapse support systems	

Planning

Use the space below to plan a 7–9 session group treatment plan. Include strategies for recruitment, monitoring and ongoing support.

Will you have a break?

Will you invite outside speakers (to talk about relaxation, activity, pharmacology etc.)?

If so, who and why?

Speaker 1
Why?

Which session?

Speaker 2
Why?

Which session?

Speaker 3
Why?

Which session?

Speaker 4
Why?

Which session?

Speaker 5
Why?

Which session?

Recruitment strategy

What?

Where?

When?

How?

Monitoring strategy

What?

Where?

When?

How?

Ongoing support

What?

Where?

When?

How?

Session 1
What will you cover?

How?

Session 2
What?

How?

Session 3
What?

How?

Session 4
What?

How?

Session 5
What?

How?

Session 6
What?

How?

References

Anderson, C., Blenkinsopp, A. and Armstrong, M. (2003) *Report 1 – The Contribution of Community Pharmacists to Improving the Public's Health. Evidence From the UK Peer Reviewed Literature 1990–2001.* Pharmacy HealthLink and Royal Pharmaceutical Society, London.

Asghar, M., Jackson, C. and Corbett, J. (2002) Specialist pharmacists in public health: are they the missing link in England? *Pharmaceutical Journal*, **268**, 22–5.

ASH (1999) *Passive Smoking.* Action on Smoking and Health, London.

ASH (2006) http://www.ash.org.uk/html/conduct/html/tobexpld3.html. Retrieved 8 January 2007.

Association of the British Pharmaceutical Industry (ABPI) (1999/2000) *Compendium of Data Sheets and Summaries of Product Characteristics.* Datapharm Publications, London.

Boreham, R. and Shaw, A. (2003) *Smoking, Drinking and Drug Use Among Young People.* Department of Health, London.

Bowman, W. C. and Rand, M. J. (1980) *Textbook of Pharmacology.* Blackwell Scientific Publications, London.

Breslau, N., Peterson, E., Schultz, L., Chilcoat, H. and Andreski, P. (1998) Major depression and stages of smoking. A longitudinal investigation. *Archives of General Psychiatry*, **55**, 161–6.

British Medical Journal (2001) *Clinical Evidence*, Issue 6. BMJ Publications, London.

Buchanan, D. and Huczynski, A. (1985) *Organisational Behaviour.* Prentice Hall, London.

Committee on Safety of Medicines (2001) Letter from chairman of CSM: Zyban-modified dosage and safety precautions. Accessed at: http://www.ash.org.uk/.

Coultard, M., Farrell, M., Singleton, N. and Meltzer, H. (2000) *Tobacco, Alcohol and Drug Use and Mental Health.* Stationery Office, London.

Croghan, E., Aveyard, P., Griffin, C. and Cheng, K. K. (2003) The importance of social sources of cigarettes to school pupils. *Tobacco Control*, **12**, 67–73.

Department of Health (1998) *Smoking Kills: a White Paper.* HMSO, London.

Department of Health (2003) *A Vision for Pharmacy in the New NHS.* Department of Health, London.

Department of Health (2004a) *Drug use, smoking and drinking among young people in England in 2003.* Department of Health, London.

Department of Health (2004b) *10 High Impact Changes for Service Improvement and Delivery.* Department of Health, London.

Department of Health (2004c) *Choosing Health, Making Healthier Choices Easier.* Department of Health, London.

Department of Health (2005) *Implementing the New Community Contractual Framework – Information for PCTs.* Department of Health, London.

GlaxoSmithKline (2001) *Summary of Product Characteristics.* Zyban 150 mg tablets. Bupropion HCl SR.

Hajek, P., Stead, L. F., West, R., Jarvis, M. and Lancaster T. (2005) Relapse prevention interventions for smoking cessation. *Cochrane Database of Systematic Reviews*, Issue 1. Art. No. CD003999.

Health Development Agency (1999) *Public Service Agreements (PSA)*. HMSO, London.

Health Development Agency (2003) *Smoking and Public Health: a Review of the Evidence*. http://www.hda.nhs.uk/documents/smoking_evidence_briefing.pdf.

Health Education Authority (1993) *Helping People Change Manual*. Health Education Authority, London.

Henrik, R. (1980) *The Psychotherapy Handbook*. New American Library, New York.

Heron, J. (1990) *Helping The Client. A Creative Practical Guide*. Sage, London.

Hughes, J. R. (1992) Tobacco withdrawal in self-quitters. *Journal of Consulting and Clinical Psychology*, **60**, 689–97.

Hughes, J. R. and Hatsukami, D. K. (1986) Signs and symptoms of tobacco withdrawal. *Archives of General Psychiatry*, **43**, 289–94.

Hughes, J. R., Higgins, S. T. and Bickel, W. K. (1994) Nicotine withdrawal versus other drug withdrawal syndromes: similarities and dissimilarities. *Addiction*, **89**, 1461–70.

Jarvis, L. (1997) *Smoking Among Secondary School Children in 1996: England*. Stationery Office, London.

Jones, L. (1994) *The Social Context of Health and Health Work*. Macmillan, London.

Jorenby, D. E., Leischow, S. J., Nides, M. A. *et al.* (1999) A controlled trial of sustained-release bupropion, a nicotine patch, or both for smoking cessation. *New England Journal of Medicine*, **340**, 685–91.

Kotler, P. and Zaltman, G. (1971) Social marketing: an approach to planned social change. *Journal of Marketing*, **35**(3), 3–12.

Kruk, Z. L. and Pycock, C. J. (1979) *Neurotransmitters and Drugs*. Croom Helm, London.

Lawn, S. and Pols, R. (2005) Smoking bans in psychiatric inpatient settings? A review of the research. *Australian and New Zealand Journal of Psychiatry*, **39**(10), 866.

MacFadyen, L., Stead, M. and Hastings, G. B. (1999) Social marketing. In: *The Marketing Book*, 4th edn (ed. M. J. Baker, Chapter 25. Butterworth-Heinemann, Oxford.

Marcus, B. H., Lewis, B. A., Hogan, J., King, T. K., Albrecht, A. E., Bock, B., Parisi, A. F., Niaura, R. and Abrams, D. B. (2005) The efficacy of moderate-intensity exercise as an aid for smoking cessation in women: a randomized controlled trial. *Nicotine & Tobacco Research*, **7**(6), 871–80.

Miller, W. and Rollnick, S. (1991) *Motivational Interviewing Preparing People to Change Addictive Behaviour*. Guilford Press, New York.

National Institute for Clinical Effectiveness (2002) Technology Appraisal Guidance No. 38: Nicotine Replacement Therapy (NRT) and Bupropion for Smoking Cessation. National Institute of Health and Clinical Effectiveness, London.

National Institute of Health and Clinical Effectiveness (2006) *Smoking Cessation. Brief Interventions and Referral for Smoking Cessation in Primary Care and Other Settings*. Available at: http://www.nice.org.uk/guidance/PHI1.

Pauli, M. (2006) http://commentisfree.guardian.co.uk/michelle_pauli/2006/06/yeuch_a_bedtime_story.html. Retrieved 8 January 2007.

Perkins, D. F. (2001) *Adolescence: the Four Questions*. Fact Sheet FCS 2117, Department of Family, Youth and Community Sciences, Florida Cooperative Extension Service, Institute of Food and Agricultural Sciences, University of Florida.

Peters, R.H. (1993). Relapse prevention approaches in the criminal justice system. In: *Relapse Prevention and the Substance-Abusing Criminal Offender*. (eds. T. T. Gorski, J. M. Kelley, L. Havens and R. H. Peters). US Department of Health and Human Services, Center for Substance Abuse Treatment.

Prochaska, J. and DiClemente, C. (1983) Stages and processes of self-change of smoking: towards an integrated model of change. *Journal of Consulting and Clinical Psychology*, **51**, 390-5.

Raw, M., McNeill, A. and West, R. (1998) Smoking cessation guidelines for health professionals. A guide to effective smoking cessation interventions for the health care system. *Thorax*, **53**(suppl. 5, Pt 1), S1–19.

Rollnick, S., and Miller, W. R. (1995) What is motivational interviewing? *Behavioural and Cognitive Psychotherapy*, 23, 325–34.

Royal College of Physicians (2000) *Nicotine Addition in Britain*. Royal College of Physicians, London.

Royal Pharmaceutical Society (1996) *Martindale: Extra Pharmacopoeia*, 31st edn. Pharmaceutical Press, London.

Trease, G. E. and Evans, C. E. (1980) *Pharmacognosy*. Baillière Tindall, Chichester.

United States Department of Health and Human Services (1989) *Reducing the Health Consequences of Smoking: 25 Years of Progress. A Report of the Surgeon General*. United States Department of Health and Human Services.

Ussher, M., West, R., McEwen, A., Taylor, A. and Steptoe, A. (2003) Efficacy of exercise counselling as an aid for smoking cessation: a randomized controlled trial. *Addiction*, **98**(4), 523–32. http://eprints.ucl.ac.uk/archive/00000341/01/add2.pdf.

Wagner, E. H., Curry, S. J., Grothaus, L., Saunders, K. W. and McBride, C. M. (1995) The impact of smoking and quitting on health care use. Archives of Internal Medicine, **155**(16), 1789–95.

West, R., McNeill, A. and Raw, M. (2003) *Meeting Department of Health Smoking Cessation Targets: Recommendations for Primary Care Trusts*. Health Development Agency, London.

West, R., McNeill, A. and Raw, M. (2000) Smoking cessation guidelines for health professionals: an update. *Thorax*, **55**, 987–9.

Wewers, M. E., Stillman, F. A., Hartman, A. M. and Shopland, D. R. (2003) Distribution of daily smokers by stage of change: Current Population Survey results. *Preventive Medicine*, **36**, 710–20.

World Health Organization (1997) *Tobacco or health: a global status report*. World Health Organization, Geneva.

World Health Organization (2002) *World Health Organization Briefing*, Geneva, 23 October.

Zevin, S. and Benowitz, N. L. (1999) Drug interactions with tobacco smoking. An update. *Clinical Pharmacokinetics*, **36**(6), 425–38.

Index